Day by Day with Mary

Day by Day with Mary

PATRICK MORAN, EDITOR

Our Sunday Visitor, Inc.
Huntington, Indiana

Nihil Obstat:
Rev. John M. Kuzmich
Censor Librorum

Imprimatur:
✠ William E. McManus, D.D.
Bishop of Fort Wayne-South Bend
April 8, 1983

ISBN: 0-87973-613-5
Library of Congress Catalog Number: 83-60101

Cover Design by OSV Graphics

Published, printed and bound in U.S.A. by
Our Sunday Visitor, Inc.
Noll Plaza
Huntington, Indiana 46750

613

Contents

Nov. 1, 27/ Dec. 4, 23
FITZGERALD, Maurus, O.F.M./ Sept. 14/ Nov. 22
FOY, Felician A., O.F.M./ Mar. 6/ May 17/ June 23/ July 20/ Aug. 22/ Oct. 12, 24/ Nov. 6
FRANCIS, Dale/ Mar. 8/ June 17/ Nov. 18/ Dec. 25

G
GINN, Roman, O.C.S.O./ Mar. 2/ Nov. 12
GORMAN, Most Rev. Thomas K./ Aug. 5, 16
GRUTKA, Most. Rev. Andrew G./ Feb. 27/ Aug. 30/ Oct. 11
GUSTAFSON, G. Joseph, S.S./ Mar. 3, 13/ Apr. 7, 29/ June 18/ July 10/ Oct. 13, 31/ Dec. 3, 24

H
HALLINAN, Most Rev. Paul J./ May 20, 25/ Sept. 11
HARTMAN, Rev. Ralph/ Jan. 15/ Oct. 5/ Dec. 18
HENNRICH, Kilian, O.F.M. Cap./ Apr. 30
HILL, Ann/ May 5
HOGAN, Joseph F., S.J./ Sept. 7

I
ILLIES, Rev. Wilfred/ July 4

K
KAISER, Edwin G., C.PP.S./ Sept. 8, 15
KENNEDY, Rev. Msgr. John S./ Mar. 18
KENZ, Sr. Carol Ann, C.S.J./ Apr. 6/ Dec. 30
KOCHER, Paul/ Apr. 5
KOWALSKI, Most Rev. Rembert, O.F.M./ Mar. 28/ July 15, 31/ Sept. 16
KUTZ, Rev. Msgr. Ralph G./ Mar. 4/ June 16, 30/ July 12/ Aug. 20/ Oct. 18/ Nov. 14

L
LARKIN, Francis, SS.CC./ July 23
LAUENSTEIN, Gary, C.SS.R./ Feb. 23
LAYNE, Marie/ Jan. 25/ Feb. 1/ Mar. 15/ Apr. 16/ June 24/ July 21/ Sept. 5/ Oct. 17, 27/ Nov. 26

LEE, Robert G. / Sept. 27
LEUVER, Robert J., C.M.F./ Jan. 28/ May 16/ Sept. 24
LOUIS, Conrad, O.S.B./ Jan. 27/ July 8
LUX, Rev. Msgr. Joseph B./ June 11/ Aug. 4/ Sept. 23

M
McCARTHY, Rev. John/ Feb. 15
McCORRY, Vincent P., S.J./ Mar. 17/ July 26/ Aug. 3, 8
McDEVITT, Edwin R., M.M./ Mar. 19/ July 1/ Sept. 4, 21/ Oct. 22/ Nov. 7/ Dec. 19
McKENZIE, Rev. Leon/ Jan. 11/ May 6
McKUNE, Rev. Msgr. J. William/ Jan. 31/ Apr. 26/ June 14/ July 7
MADDEN, Richard, O.C.D./ Jan. 29/ Feb. 6
MAGUIRE, Rev. John R./ July 25/ Aug. 25/ Nov. 4
MALLON, Vincent P., M.M./ Oct. 29
MALLOY, Most Rev. William T./ Apr. 19
MALSAM, Margaret Hula/ Feb. 24/ Mar. 9/ Apr. 11, 22/ Aug. 28
MANTON, Joseph E., C.SS.R./ Jan. 17/ Feb. 18/ Apr. 10/ June 27/ July 3
MARLING, Most. Rev. Joseph M., C.PP.S./ July 5/ Aug. 23
MARTIN, John M., M.M./ Mar. 12/ May 18/ Dec. 12
MARTIN, Terry/ Feb. 26/ June 3/ Oct. 10
MARTIN, Tom, S.J./ Jan. 22/ May 13/ Aug. 2
MAUREEN, Sr. Mary, S.S.J./ Jan. 26/ Aug. 24
MEEHAN, Robert/ Feb. 7
MERZ, Linus, S.C.J./ Feb. 11/ May 8
MILLER, Donald F., C.SS.R./ Feb. 16
MOESLEIN, Rev. Francis R./ Aug. 14/ Oct. 14
MOLPHY, Sr. Theresa, C.S.J./ Apr. 28/ Sept. 20/ Dec. 22
MORAN, Patrick R./ May 14, 22
MURPHY, Eugene P., S.J./ Feb. 28
MURRAY, Albert A., C.S.P./ May 26, 30/ Aug. 10/ Sept. 3
MYERS, Rev. Rawley/ Jan. 13/ Feb. 14/ Mar. 11/ June 10, 13/ July

19/ Aug. 7/ Sept. 29/ Nov. 25

N

NEIDHART, William J., C.S.C./ Apr. 2/ May 21

NEVINS, Albert J., M.M./ Nov. 3

NIMETH, Albert J., O.F.M./ Jan. 18/ Feb. 10/ Mar. 26/ Apr. 14/ June 26/ July 29/ Aug. 17/ Oct. 25/ Nov. 5, 30/ Dec. 14

NOLAN, Rev. Msgr. John G./ June 7/ Sept. 1

NUSBAUM, James M., S.J./ Nov. 10

O

O'BRIEN, Rev. John A./June 15/ Aug. 13/ Sept. 17

O'MALLEY, Rev. Msgr. Edward W./ Feb. 8

O'NEILL, Anne/ Feb. 19/ Apr. 21/ July 22

P

PERRY, Norman, O.F.M./ Feb. 2/ Aug. 21./ Nov. 16

PEYTON, Patrick, C.S.C./ Aug. 18/ Oct. 1/ Nov. 8

PINGER, Most Rev. Henry A., O.F.M./ Jan. 20/ June 5

POLZIN, Theresita/ Feb. 13/ Apr. 8/ July 13

POWER, Albert, S.J./ Feb. 9

PURSLEY, Most Rev. Leo A./ Jan. 23/ Feb. 3/ Mar. 22/ July 11/ Oct. 6

PUTZ, Louis J., C.S.C./ Nov. 15

R

RAMGE, Sebastian V., O.C.D./ Mar. 21/ Apr. 9/ Oct. 21

RAYMOND, M., O.C.S.O./ Nov. 21, 29

RISKI, Bruce, O.F.M. Cap. / Jan. 19/ June 2/ Aug. 11/ Dec. 5

ROGERS, Peter V., O.M.I./ Apr. 18/ Aug. 26/ Dec. 29

ROXBURGH, Gilbert, O.P./ Sept. 30

RUSSELL, Dianne/ May 27

S

SCHAUER, Blase, O.P./ Nov. 19

SCHOENBERG, Martin, O.S.C./ June 12

SCHOTT, Valerian, O.F.M./ Feb. 22

SELNER, John C., S.S./ Feb. 29/ July 14, 30/ Aug. 12

SHEEN, Most Rev. Fulton J./ Jan. 9/ Apr. 13/ Dec. 27

SHINE, Bernardine, O.S.B./ Feb. 4

SIGUR, Rev. Msgr. Alexander/ Jan. 8

SMITH, Most Rev. Leo R./ Jan. 7

SPELGATTI, Rev. Msgr. David P./ Mar. 23/ July 17

STEFANCIC, Jane J./ Oct. 19

STEVENS, Rev. Clifford/ Mar. 16/ Apr. 15, 27/ May 19/ Aug. 27/ Nov. 28

STRAVINSKAS, Rev. Mr. Peter/ Jan. 14/ May 31

SULLIVAN, James Michael/ Apr. 17/ Oct. 15

T

TANSEY, Anne/ May 3, 23/ June 4, 29/ Sept. 19/ Oct. 3, 20/ Dec. 13, 31

TOBIN, Rev. Msgr. Thomas J./ Dec. 8

TOURNIER, Rev. Msgr. Francis/ Dec. 9, 17

TRESE, Rev. Leo J./ June 6

TUCEK, Rev. Msgr. James I./ May 15/ June 1/ Aug. 29

V

VAUGHAN, Joseph A., S.J./ Oct. 8

W

WELP, Rev. Msgr. Harry J./ Mar. 14/ June 28

WILKEN, Rev. Robert L./ April 24/ Dec. 6

Y

YZERMANS, Rev. Vincent A./ Mar. 10/ Aug. 15/ Oct. 16/ Dec. 2

Z

ZUROWESTE, Most Rev. Albert R./ May 28/ Sept. 9

Introduction

DAY BY DAY WITH MARY is a collection of Marian thoughts and themes selected from issues of the 25-year-old MY DAILY VISITOR magazine. This anthology contains 366 spiritual and inspirational reflections written by 134 outstanding Church leaders, religious, scholars, authors, editors, radio and television personalities.

The calendar date and the name of the feast day, or special Marian observance, leads off each daily entry. Source of this special feature is "Our Lady's Calendar," provided and printed with permission from Rev. Stanley Matuszewski, M.S., Editor of *Our Lady's Digest.* This quarterly national Marian review is published at Twin Lakes, Wisconsin.

Insofar as possible the reflections and meditations are coordinated with the Marian calendar events of the day. Other entries, however, contain general inspirational thoughts of a Marian nature. Concluding the reflection is a prayer or thought line consisting of many familiar, aspirations and fervorinos.

A collection of prayers to the Blessed Virgin Mary is also featured with each daily entry. They are presented in a run-on fashion — as one prayer line or thought per day. Familiar Marian prayers and the dates in which they begin, are:

Litany of Loreto, Jan. 1; Litany of the Immaculate Heart of Mary, Feb. 25; Prayer of Intercession to Mary, July 1; Marian Prayer, July 23; Angelic Salutation, Aug. 1; Hail, Holy Queen, Aug. 8; Ave Regina Caelorum, Aug. 21; The Memorare, Sept. 1; The Angelus, Sept. 17; Regina Coeli, Oct. 1; Marian Prayer, Oct. 19; The Magnificat, Nov. 1; An Evening Prayer (Alma Redemptoris Mater), Nov. 19; To Mary, Our Hope, Dec. 1.

The Marian monogram is graphically interspersed throughout these pages. The monogram was designed by intertwining the five initials or letters forming the name Maria. This emblem is also the original symbol for Miriam, the Hebrew name for Mary. Elsewhere, readers are sure to notice the photo accompanying a poetic reflection in the entry for April 20. (This graphic concept of Our Lady was captured by John Zierten, graphics director, Our Sunday Visitor, Inc.) A pastel tile mosaic wall provides the backdrop for a life-sized statue of the Blessed Virgin Mary, overlooking a reflective pool amid plantings and flowers in the landscaped patio at Noll Plaza.

The following citation in 1954 by the then Bishop Amleto G. Cicognani, former Apostolic Delegate to the United States, captures the overall essence of DAY BY DAY WITH MARY, with these words:

"Mary, more than any other woman, has received homage for literature, oratory, poetry, painting, sculpture, and music. She is unquestionably the most titled personage who ever lived. To what other woman have been dedicated so many churches, shrines, chapels, sanctuaries, and monuments?"

Although Mary is honored with more than 2,300 titles, I uncovered 719 various Marian reflections appearing in MY DAILY VISITOR since its inception, February 1957. MDV contributors or Guest Editors numbered 134, and they drew from the many inspirational thoughts and beautiful insights of historic and contemporary Marian writers.

This book's theme is quite evident. The Rosary shows us the way — to Jesus through Mary!

Patrick Moran
Editor
MY DAILY VISITOR

JANUARY

□ 1 □

Solemnity of Mary the Mother of God

The *Constitution on the Church* (Second Vatican Council) has a wonderful chapter on our Blessed Mother titled: "The Blessed Virgin Mary, Mother of God, in the Mystery of Christ and the Church." Although the chapter does not pretend to offer a complete doctrine on Mary, it does, as the title indicates, describe her role in the Church and our duties toward her.

"In conceiving Christ, in bringing Him forth, in nourishing Him, in presenting Him to the Father in the temple, in suffering with Him as He died on the cross, Mary cooperated in the work of salvation in an altogether singular way, in obedience, faith, hope and burning charity, to restore supernatural life to souls. As a result, she is our Mother in the order of grace" (61).

Our Blessed Mother stands at the center of both the Old and the New Testament. We might put it this way: Christ was the perfect response to the love of God the Father for man. And after Christ, no one cooperated so fully with God's plan as did Mary. We need her intercession now perhaps more than ever before, so let us put ourselves into the hands of Mary, who represents the beauty of the Church, the bride of Christ.

Holy Mary—pray for us.

SISTER ELIZABETH ANN CLIFFORD, O.L.V.M.

□ 2 □

Our Lady of the Pillar — Saragossa, Spain

How lovely is our Lady! Her large and beautiful eyes could tell a thousand tales. Her hands could sketch the deepest love of all the earth. Her heart could enclose the whole of creation. Her "yes" has filled the silent void of eternal peace.

Blessed is she because she believed, because she heard the Father call her name; and she never doubted that she could respond. Blessed is she because she has been a mother—and blessed are all mothers in her. Blessed is Mary, the virgin, because she touched the pulse of never ending love.

She did not have to say yes! She did not have to heed the call of her Father, except insofar as she was prepared to be holy. She didn't have to endure such sorrow as she did, but for her love of God and His love for her. But she did say "yes." She did heed His call, and she did suffer sorrow. And that has made all the difference.

O lovely Mother, we look to you as a model of womanhood and holiness. You are the honor and glory of your people.

Holy Mother of God—pray for us.

T. TIMOTHY DELANEY

□ 3 □

Madonna of Sichem—Central Palestine

Do we ever think of thanking God for the wonderful gifts He has given Mary? Such an attempt on our part touches her heart very much, and is very pleasing to her and to God.

After all, she is God's Masterpiece, and He deserves our congratulations on His work. She has never ceased trying to thank God for her wonderful privileges: for the love of the Holy Spirit for her, for her Immaculate Conception, for her wonderful vocation, for her Assumption—for everything.

She is very appreciative of our help, and will not remain long in our debt without making a regal repayment.

Holy Virgin of virgins—pray for us.

EUGENE BOYLAN, O.C.S.O

JANUARY

□ 4 □

Our Lady of Treves—Germany

In speaking of our Lady, Cardinal John Henry Newman stressed the distinction between what our *faith* teaches concerning her and our *devotion* to her. He wrote:

"By 'faith,' I mean the Creed and the assent to the Creed; by 'devotion,' I mean . . . religious honors and the payment of those honors. Faith and devotion are as distinct in fact, as they are in idea."

What faith teaches about Mary will ever be the same, for it is given to us by Holy Mother the Church and handed down to us in the writings of the Fathers. These teachings are mines, whence we increase our knowledge of Mary; and from that knowledge our love and devotion, according to each individual's reaction, will be expressed.

Our faith has so much to give us, from which our devotion can grow sound and deep. From both, we will become truly children of Mary, and sense her loving protection.

Mother of Christ—pray for us.

MOST REV. JOHN J. CARBERRY

□ 5 □

Our Lady of Prosperity—France

Devotion to the Blessed Mother is always the sign of a fervent Christian, a devout Catholic. Where love of Mary flourishes, there is always a deep appreciation of Jesus Christ, the God-man.

The reason for our devotion to the Blessed Virgin is very simple. God has chosen her first. His grace is mighty in her. She is the vessel of election chosen to bring the Christ into the world. What greater honor could there be?

The Holy Spirit inspired her to prophesy: "Behold, all generations shall call me blessed." Every time we use that "blessed" title for Mary, we are simply fulfilling what has been foretold from the beginning of Christianity. And how correct—Mary is the first Christian!

Mother of divine grace—pray for us.

REV. CHARLES DOLLEN

JANUARY

□ 6 □

First Miracle of Our Lord
Through Mary's Intercession at Cana

At a wedding in Galilee (John 2.1-12), much depended on the wine. But now the wine was running low. To prevent the embarrassment that empty wine jars would cause, Mary, the Mother of Jesus, intervened and said to her Son: "They have no wine." She did not ask for a miracle. She simply made known a pressing need and left the rest to His discretion—an admirable way of praying.

To the waiters, Mary said: "Do whatever He tells you." Those are the last words of the Mother of God recorded in the Gospels. The changing of water into the wine at Cana was the first of a long series of benefits that mankind has obtained from the providence of God through the intervention of the Blessed Virgin Mary.

Mother most pure—pray for us.

THOMAS M. BREW, S.J.

□ 7 □

Return of Our Lady from Egypt
with Jesus and Joseph

The Word of God came to St. Joseph as a command: "Fear not to take unto thee Mary thy wife." Later again: "Arise, take the child and his mother, and flee into Egypt." And again: "Arise, take the child and his mother, and go into the land of Israel." Finally, "Knew ye not that I must needs be in my Father's house?"

Each time, great self-sacrifice was demanded of St. Joseph, but he accepted each word humbly and carried it out. If I am young, do I do what I am told by my father and mother? If I am grown, do I carry out the duties of my calling in life humbly and faithfully, like St. Joseph? Do I accept the Commandments of God, not in a sullen way, but gladly, as the desires of my God?

"It seems to me that to other saints our Lord has given power to help us in only one kind of necessity; but the glorious St. Joseph, I know by experience, assists us in all kinds of necessities"—St. Teresa of Avila.

Mother most chaste—pray for us.

MOST REV. LEO R. SMITH

JANUARY

□ 8 □

Our Lady of Prompt Succor—New Orleans, Louisiana

In Louisiana, Catholics observe the day as the feast of Our Lady of Prompt Succor, patroness of the state. It was through her miraculous intervention that the city of New Orleans was saved from fire and capture by British forces in the Battle of New Orleans, 1815.

Catholics everywhere need the pattern of our Lady, and that of St. Paul the Hermit—in quiet, recollected prayer. We are all too tense. We are a living lie to the spiritual nature of man as we rush to bodily comfort, mechanical gadgetry, physical exertion in the extreme.

We run to and fro, with little concern for the spirit. Mary, however, "kept all these things in her heart, pondering them." Paul the Hermit spent ninety years in solitude—him we can only admire, not imitate—in adoration and contemplation.

Meditation, mental prayer, conversation with Christ—call it what you will—we need it. How can we do the work of the Lord if we do not know His mind? Let us speak with Him, today.

Mother inviolate—pray for us.

REV. MSGR. ALEXANDER SIGUR

□ 9 □

Our Lady Beyond the Tiber—Rome

From the moment when the Blessed Mother pronounced her *fiat*, from the day when the Son of God took a human nature to save humanity, God has willed that humanity be saved through man. As a diamond is polished with diamond dust, so man is converted through man. Christ has no other hands with which to aid the poor but our own.

Because it is humanity that He was to save, and not us alone in our own country, then our love must be as catholic as we are Catholic. "Go ye into the whole world." If Jerusalem had said: "We must make everyone here a follower of Christ before we convert Rome," Rome would never have the faith. If Rome had said: " We must convert all our pagans before we send Patrick to Ireland, Cyril and Methodius to Baltic lands, or Boniface to Germany," these countries would never have had the faith.

The Catholic who is not preoccupied with the world is not truly Catholic, and it is only by saving the world for Christ that we save our own lands.

Mother undefiled—pray for us.

MOST REV. FULTON J. SHEEN

□ 10 □

Our Lady of Guides

The Virgin Mother, who brought us Christ and is herself the most perfect mirror of Christ, is the closest external link we have with Christ, and as such is the most powerful of all influences in keeping us close to Christ. This is the role of her divine maternity, formulated by God as His means of manifesting His Son to the world. She shows us Christ, and she knows what we need to make us conformable to the image of Christ. Nobody could know better: she is His Mother.

Mary is also our Mother. The soul's need of a heavenly Mother intimately united to God is much greater than that of an earthly mother faithfully groping for God. The soul is helped in the same vital way by the same maternal functions, transformed, transfigured, and performed on the heavenly plane. In the search for Christ, the soul needs the Mother of Christ. In the struggle to know and practice the virtues of Christ, the soul needs the Mother of Divine Grace.

In its falls from Christ, the soul needs the refuge it finds in the Mother of Mercy. In the sacrifices and sorrows it undergoes for Christ, it needs the support of the Mother of Sorrows. In the understanding of, and adherence to, the lofty ideals of Christ, it needs the perfect reflection of them that it finds in the Immaculate Heart of Mary—the Virgin, the Queen, and the Mother.

Mother most amiable—pray for us.

MOST REV. RICHARD J. CUSHING

□ 11 □

Notre Dame de Bessiere—Limousin, France

The painters, in ages past, frequently tried to capture on canvas the *inwardness* of two types of women, the virgin and the mother. Through the centuries, artists have labored to portray the freshness and delicacy of virginal purity, the glow that is the luminescence of untouched innocence. And no less have they attempted to depict the dignity and warmth of motherhood. Is it any wonder that there have been so many paintings of Mary and her divine Son? Artists have been imitating the great artistry of the divine Artist.

In Mary, God produced a work of art that combined the seeming contradictories of virginity and maternity. In Mary, God portrayed the fragile beauty of virginal purity and the tender charm of maternity. In Mary, God summed up the most admirable of all womanly qualities.

Mother most admirable—pray for us.

REV. LEON MC KENZIE

□ 12 □

Madonna of the Rue Large—Rome

In a crowded Roman street, there is a rather striking shrine of our Lady, built into the wall of a Carmelite convent. It shows an image of Mary in mosaic, with the title: "O Virgin Mary, Mother of Divine Love, make us saints."

There is so much food for thought in this prayer. Mary is the Mother of Jesus, the Son of God, whose heart burned with divine love for us.

The plea—"make us saints"—does not come easily to our lips. Yet St. Paul wrote, "This is the will of God—your sanctification." When we ask to be saints, we are not seeking to be extraordinary. No, we ask simply to do God's holy will in our lives, to keep ourselves in the state of grace, and to have the love of Christ fill our hearts. Holiness is the real happiness of life.

Mother of good counsel—pray for us.

MOST REV. JOHN J. CARBERRY

□ 13 □

Our Lady of Virtues—Verdun;
*Little Office of the Blessed Virgin ***

St. Pius V was a Dominican priest living in a very difficult time in history. The ferocious Turks were set on invading Europe and

* Revised by Pope Pius V in 1571.

destroying its Christian civilization. He called on the people of Europe to get down on their knees and pray the Rosary to save their land. The people responded everywhere, and, miraculously, a small Christian fleet was able to turn back the large Turkish armada.

A saintly pope like Pius V knew the need for prayer. Prayer is the greatest thing we do in life. As the Trappist monk Thomas Merton wrote, "Nothing good happens in this world without prayer." The people of Europe on their knees saved Christianity.

In our life, prayer is vital also. It is the most important thing that we do. People who are too busy to pray—are too busy. We must pray, or perish. There is too little prayer today: that is the reason for so many of our problems. When we pray, Christ is with us. If Christ is with us, we can overcome all things.

Mother of our Creator—pray for us.

REV. RAWLEY MYERS

□ 14 □

Our Lady of Speech—Montserrat, Spain; Birth of St. Bernadette

The great events in history came about through a word. God spoke, and the beauties of creation began to unfold. Mary spoke her "Let it be . . .," and God became man. The Church speaks a word of memory, and bread and wine are transformed into the risen Christ.

A word is powerful. A word can be creative or destructive. Before this day ends, each of us will have spoken hundreds of words. Let us resolve to make them words of love, support, and encouragement.

Mother of our Savior—pray for us.

REV. MR. PETER STRAVINSKAS

□ 15 □

Our Lady of the Crops—Syria

During the reign of recent popes, papal visitation has become a happy commonplace. In contrast to former eras, the reigning pontiff chooses to travel beyond the confines of the Vatican on various occasions. These have proved to be events of international import.

JANUARY

Another kind of visit had been going on during all those years when the pope was the "prisoner of the Vatican." These were visits by our Lady—visits that were occasions of great concern.

Before the time comes when we must qualify the expression "these United States," Americans ought to look to their Patroness and ask her intercession on behalf of this land of "amber grain . . . purple mountains . . . and fruited plain." America's approach to the rest of the world makes her unique: she is mother to the world's homeless and the vindication of the world's dreams. Keep her thus, Mary!

Virgin most prudent—pray for us.

REV. RALPH HARTMAN

□ 16 □

Our Lady, Refuge of Sinners—Congregation of the Holy Ghost and of the Immaculate Heart of Mary

Jesus came to save sinners. Mary's mind has always been in accord with that of her beloved Son. She is called Refuge of Sinners because of her undying love for all the children of God.

Holy Mary has always come to the aid of sinners, helping them to avoid the pitfalls of serious sin, which could lead to permanent damage to their souls. She knows that purity can come with proper understanding. No matter what sin is committed, she will intercede for the sinner. Prayers and devotions of seekers with a sincere attitude will bear fruit.

We should entrust the conversion of a sinner to Mary's hands — never losing hope, never despairing, no matter how grave the situation. We can be assured that all the saints of the Church will aid Mary's rescue mission on behalf of a troubled sinner.

Virgin most venerable—pray for us.

JOHN JULIUS FISHER

□ 17 □

Notre Dame de Pontmain

At first, God presented Himself to mankind only by promise. But after the Fall, He came upon earth and took man by the hand. Human happiness and salvation lay in ruins, but those who lived amidst this desolation gazed into the distance and watched the approach of the City of God. God had inflicted a heavy punishment upon them, but it was tempered by the gracious possibility of reconciliation. Eve sat before the locked gate of the Paradise she had lost; but now God also set Mary before the gate.

Truly the Church is Our Lady's Cathedral, a cathedral in which Mary herself is the altar. It is like a church prepared for Mass. The altar is ready, the candles are lighted, the bells summon the faithful. . . . Christ has not yet appeared, but He will come!

We fall at the Virgin's feet, before the gates of God's city; we crouch there like a beggar, knocking at the door of her heart, asking that she may open those gates of life to us. — Bishop Ottokar Prohaszka, *Meditations on the Gospels.*

Virgin most renowned—pray for us.

JOSEPH E. MANTON, C.SS.R.

□ 18 □

Our Lady of Dijon—France

Devotion to Mary does not necessarily consist of beautiful music, special services, and gorgeous shrines. These may stimulate and foster devotion, but they are external and do not constitute devotion. Sweet sentiment and fine feeling likewise do not constitute devotion to Mary. These come and go, and are not always under our control. Devotion is deliberate and endures. It does not fluctuate with our mood. It does not disappear when we are hungry and return after a satisfying meal.

Conviction is the basis for devotion. We are convinced that Mary does have a unique position in God's plan of salvation. This conviction reveals itself not only by our having recourse to her, but also by our making a serious attempt to imitate the virtues prominent in the life of Mary—and thus making our own the same mission she fulfilled. This mission is not accomplished by sporadic attempts, whims of the moment. It is a steady, lifelong endeavor.

Virgin most powerful—pray for us.

ALBERT J. NIMETH, O.F.M.

JANUARY

☐ 19 ☐

Our Lady of the Exile

No other century in the history of man has seen the flight of so many millions of people because of wars and peace treaties as the twentieth century. The mental anguish and physical pain the involuntary flights brought in their wake are incalculable. The tragic, sorrowful effects will endure for generations. Our Lady of Fatima declared that "war is a punishment for sin." The chastisement inflicted on mankind in this century has been most severe. The sins of man had become intolerable and roused God's wrath.

There was a much earlier example of flight. Joseph, warned by an angel in a dream, fled with Mary and the child Jesus into Egypt. They accepted the will of God. In time, the danger subsided, and they returned to their homeland.

By means of prayer, we can assist those who were uprooted from their homes, and perhaps bring it about, if such be God's will, that they may return to their homelands.

Virgin most merciful—pray for us.

BRUCE RISKI, O.F.M. Cap.

☐ 20 ☐

Our Lady of Tables—Montpellier

Perhaps the shortest homily on record, intended for the largest audience, was given by the Blessed Mother herself.

The Gospels reveal to us only a few of Mary's words; but of these, she addressed all mankind in her words at the wedding feast in Cana. Although she addressed them directly to a few attendants, her words were meant for all mankind.

In the various apparitions of the Blessed Mother over the centuries, she really did not say anything that was not already included in her "sermon" at Cana. To remember these words of the Blessed Mother is not difficult; to carry out her bidding is to give proof that our love for her Son is sincere. Nothing else we could do will give her greater pleasure and joy than this—to follow her motherly admonition: "Do whatever He tells you."

Virgin most faithful—pray for us.

MOST REV. HENRY A. PINGER, O.F.M. (China)

□ 21 □

Our Lady of Consolation

In our trials, our tribulations, our agonies, Jesus and His Mother can fully sympathize with us. They also knew what it meant to be exhausted, to be thirsty, to feel pain, to be lonely, to be misunderstood. They did have something special about them, though. They did not know the weakness of sin.

Instead of lamenting the sufferings our sins cause us, let us take a few minutes to consider the terrible pain our sins caused to the sinless Jesus and Mary. Any pain and any privation they suffered on earth were caused entirely by the sins of man! We will never know the full horror of sin until we understand what sin did to Christ and His blessed Mother.

Mirror of Justice—pray for us.

REV. DONALD F. X. CONNOLLY

□ 22 □

Espousals of Our Lady

St. Joseph and the Blessed Virgin had a love for each other as husband and wife. Mary helped Joseph to get to heaven, and Joseph helped Mary to get to heaven.

What did Joseph think and do when he learned of the pregnancy of Mary? Being a "just man," he decided to cause her no harm but to "put her away" without exposing her "fault." But the angel of God put Joseph straight.

Mary could not defend herself, because no one would believe her story of an angel's announcing to her that she would be the mother of the Word-made-flesh.

There are times in our life when we are confused beyond all power of explanation. Then it is that we must turn in prayer to our Lord, who knows all. We must tell our Lord prayerfully, "Lord, I do not know what to do. Help me." He speaks to us through His priests, if we ask for advice.

Seat of Wisdom—pray for us.

TOM MARTIN, S.J.

□ 23 □

Notre Dame d'Ambronay—France

We know so few of the details of Mary's life on earth, and yet, without being told, we are quite sure that she was loved by all who ever came to know her. Her friends and neighbors would look forward to seeing her; they were happy in her presence; they treasured the words that fell—so rarely—from her lips; they went away happier and stronger than when they came; they were filled with goodwill toward her, ready to do anything to serve her; and the very thought of her—the remembrance that there was such a one—added a new joy to their lives.

Then again, there have been those in more recent times who have been privileged to see Mary with their own eyes, such as the child Bernadette; and they too have always loved her on sight, as it were, even before they knew who she was.

Cause of our joy—pray for us.

MOST REV. LEO A. PURSLEY

□ 24 □

Our Lady of Peace

The simple invocation "Mary, Queen of Peace" has often proved a powerful aid to troubled souls. We have been assured that we should not worry, or go back over the past; but nevertheless, when we least expect, a nagging may come to disturb us. Other anxieties come with each day. At such times, let us humbly say, "Mary, Queen of Peace." While we say this, we should gently turn our minds toward our loving Mother, away from the cause of our worry, and ask her to fill our souls with peace.

No matter what the cause of the distress—the future, distrust of self, remorse, scruples—let "Mary, Queen of Peace" be on our lips. Mary will come to us with motherly care and balm.

Mary, Queen of Peace, fill my soul with the peace of Christ. Bless our homes with this precious peace, and bring the world to the only truly lasting peace, in Christ.

Spiritual Vessel—pray for us.

MOST REV. JOHN J. CARBERRY

JANUARY

□ 25 □

After Mary's assumption, Christ presented His Mother before the throne of the Divinity: "Eternal Father, it is right that to my Mother be given the reward of a Mother. And since during all her life and in all her works she was like to me as it is possible for a human creature to be, let her also be like to me in glory and on the Throne of Our Majesty."

The Eternal Father proclaimed: "Our Daughter Mary has been chosen by our Will from all creatures as the first in our Favor, and she has never fallen from the position of a true daughter. Therefore, she has a claim to our Kingdom, of which she is to be acknowledged and crowned the lawful sovereign and Queen."

The Incarnate Word declared: "To my true and natural Mother belong all the creatures that I have created and redeemed. Of all things over which I am King, she shall be the rightful Queen."

Then the Holy Spirit said: "By the title of my only chosen spouse, to which she has faithfully corresponded, the crown of Queen also is bestowed on her for all eternity."

Vessel of Honor—pray for us.

MARIE LAYNE

□ 26 □

Our Lady of Long-Fields—France

Listening is a skill that needs to be developed in the young — and the not so young — in our times. When this skill is a part of our daily life, it can be applied in the spiritual realm.

Mary is an example for us in so many ways. One way is the manner in which she listened. Mary listened to God in prayer and in the traditions of her people. She listened and heard Him speak in Scriptures, as is evident in her life. Her Magnificat is based on Scripture, because she listened to His word and applied it to her life. Mary listened to others also, and thereby learned to love God more deeply.

Mary used every opportunity to be more present to the Lord. She is our model as a good listener, so that we also might become more aware of God and what He tells us in His word and in His people.

Singular Vessel of Devotion—pray for us.

SISTER MARY MAUREEN, S.S.J.

JANUARY

☐ 27 ☐

Our Lady of Life—Provence, France

Mary was so perfectly *womanly*. As we know her, she was always at hand at the right time with the right word, the right deed, the right understanding.

She was always ready with a helping hand: "Be it done to me according to thy word." She wrapped the Child in swaddling clothes. She found Him in the Temple. She noticed that the bride and groom had no wine. Mary followed Jesus with timely attention during His ministry. She stood by Him at the end, compassionate in the fullest sense. Mary mothered the infant Church, as she had mothered the infant Child (Acts 1.12-14).

Don't we need more such womanly women among us today?

Mystical Rose—pray for us.

CONRAD LOUIS, O.S.B.

☐ 28 ☐

Our Lady of Succor—Rouen

In the long quiet hours of the night, those who are ill are often overwhelmed by loneliness and despair. A nurse in a large Catholic hospital made a practice of suggesting to her sleepless patients that they repeat slowly, over and over, the aspiration, "My Mother, my Confidence." This did not tax their strength, and more often than not she later found them sleeping quietly.

Even as little children, our knowing that mother was close by helped each of us through many restless nights. Our heavenly Mother's presence is much more effective, if we but call her to our bedside. She who is known as "Comforter of the Afflicted" will show us that she well deserves the title.

When passing a hospital, never neglect a prayer to our Lady, that she may help all those confined within its walls, especially the dying.

Tower of David—pray for us.

ROBERT J. LEUVER, C.M.F.

□ 29 □

It is almost impossible for us to celebrate any feast of our Lady without being grateful to her for being such a loving mother to us. It is also a good time to check ourselves on our gratitude to our earthly mothers (and fathers, for that matter).

Our parents are pretty much responsible for everything we have and are. Throughout the course of our lifetimes, they provided for our needs, watched through the night when we were sick, and suffered broken hearts at many of our indiscreet capers.

We owe our parents all the love we can muster, which should not be difficult for us. We owe them respect—and it doesn't matter how much money they have, what kind of clothes they wear, or how broken their English is. They are our parents, and nothing else counts.

God gave them to us on loan. When their work is done, God will call them back. So let's treasure them while we have them with us.

Tower of Ivory—pray for us.

RICHARD MADDEN, O.C.D.

□ 30 □

Madonna of the Rose—Lucca, Italy

"Mary is the most beautiful flower that was ever seen in the spiritual world. It is by the power of God's grace that from this barren and desolate earth there has ever sprung up flowers of holiness and glory. And Mary is Queen of them. She is the Queen of spiritual flowers; and therefore she is called the Rose, for the rose is fitly called of all flowers the most beautiful. . . .

"She is called *mystical* or the *hidden* Rose, for mystical means hidden. Is it conceivable that they who have been so reverent and careful of the bodies of the Saints and Marytrs should neglect her—the Queen of Martyrs and the Queen of Saints, who was the very Mother of the Lord? It is impossible. Why, then, is she thus the *hidden* Rose? Plainly because her sacred body is in heaven, not on earth"—Cardinal John Henry Newman, *Meditations.*

House of Gold—pray for us.

MOST REV. JOHN J. CARBERRY

JANUARY

The Hidden Life of Mary

In his book *Life of Jesus,* François Mauriac asks the question: What did Mary and Jesus talk about as they ate supper together in the little house in Nazareth? No one knows, of course. But think of the problem of faith that Mary faced.

She had not forgotten the words of Gabriel, or the adoration of the Magi, or those other events that "paid homage" to the divinity of her Son. He was to be the King of Israel, to rule in the house of David forever.

But after some thirty years had gone by, her Son had done nothing. No doubt He was a good carpenter; but He did not act like a king by any means. He showed no sign of regal aspirations.

Did Mary, after thirty years, begin to wonder about the angel's prophecy? Thirty years, and no sign of fulfillment! She was working out her salvation in the darkness of faith, like the rest of us.

Ark of the Covenant—pray for us.

REV. MSGR. J. WILLIAM MC KUNE

FEBRUARY

□ 1 □

Baptism of St. Louis de Montfort

Mary is God's treasure. God has placed all gifts and graces in her hands. God has permitted her such liberty that she gives to whomever she wills, as and when she wills, and as much as she wills. Through Mary, endless graces can flow to us. She is God's reservoir of graces. We must turn to her for the graces we need.

Through the centuries, Mary is the fountain of grace from which all may draw. Even as God has gathered all the waters to form the sea (Latin *mare*), so, St. Louis de Montfort tells us, He has made an assemblage of all His graces and called it Mary (Latin *Maria*).

Mary is cognizant of every request made to her. She prays for us and intervenes for us. She thinks of the rich, the poor, the wise, the ignorant, the sinner, and the just. Mary's prayers are all-powerful. Whenever we receive a favor, temporal or spiritual, we receive it from God through Mary, through her merciful Immaculate Heart.

Morning Star—pray for us.

MARIE LAYNE

☐ 2 ☐

Presentation of Our Lord

J oseph and Mary have come to offer their Son to the Lord. Simeon takes the infant from their hands and utters the prophecy that rings through the centuries: "This child is destined to be the downfall and rise of many in Israel, a sign that will be opposed." He will be a sign of contradiction, says Simeon. And over and over again his words prove true.

Jesus and His Gospel stand in constant opposition to the values of a world without moral values or faith in God. His warnings against love of money, comfort, and pleasure contradict the values of people seeking happiness in things and possessions. His call to care for the poor, to sacrifice, and to renounce violence "accuses" the self-centered and self-seeking. His call to chastity, purity, and fidelity convicts those who promote "open" marriage, premarital sex, cohabitation without marriage, and so forth.

Jesus, help me see in You and the Cross a constant challenge to my own values and goals in life. Grant that my life, like Yours, may also become a sign in opposition to those who reject You and the Cross.

Health of the Sick—pray for us.

NORMAN PERRY, O.F.M.

☐ 3 ☐

Our Lady of Seideneida—near Damascus

" O ur Blessed Mother, she who weeps, . . . this tremendous Mother looks upon her sons and daughters all over the world, some in the gray dungeons behind the Iron Curtain, others in the glittering prisons of the 'free world' whose iron bars are materialism, secularism, atheistic humanism, personal sin. Does she weep? Mystically she weeps, for just as the mystic sword of consecration in the Mass would slay Christ again, were He not the Risen Lord, so the vision of her belittled and degraded children would pierce the Blessed Mother's heart — were she not in glory—and renew . . . her ancient sorrows. . . .

"She who is always present by her knowledge and maternal love, the Blessed Mother appears visibly on this earth at Lourdes, at LaSalette, at Fatima. She who educated the humanity of God in Galilee has appeared

FEBRUARY

on this earth in later days and called to us her other children who have been too long absent from her wise instructions" — Frederick A. Harkins. S.J., *Mary and Modern Man.*

Refuge of Sinners—pray for us.

MOST REV. LEO A. PURSLEY

□ 4 □

Our Lady of Fire—Forli, Italy

Suffering shadows the soul with darkness. It is also a light, revealing to the soul's eyes. Darkness unveils disloyalty and unmasks fickleness. Suffering is the crucible testing the true gold of loyalty, devotion, and love.

The sacrificial flames consuming Christ were the fires proving His sorrowful Mother beneath the cross. Her hands were always open to receive heaven's gifts. Her heart was never closed to giving. In her virginal womb, Mary accepted God's gift of His Son. She embraced the fullness of her mother's vocation: joy in receiving, sorrow in giving. Her Son was now saving His people from their sins. Heroically she stood near Him while the bitter waters overflowing the fountain of the cross drenched her soul.

Our love becomes strong and selfless in giving to Christ, not always receiving from Him. Fidelity to our share of the cross is fidelity in fulfilling our vocation.

Comforter of the Afflicted—pray for us.

BERNARDINE SHINE, O.S.B.

□ 5 □

Dedication of the First Church of Our Lady
by St. Peter—Tripoli

"Mary, in her own life, lived an example of that maternal love by which all should be fittingly animated who cooperate in the apostolic mission of the Church on behalf of the rebirth of men" (Vatican II).

Manner of life and manner of mission are inseparable and interdependent. There can be mission without love, and love without mission; but the one will be cold and the other static. Love is good and mission is good. Bring them together and you have this: "God loved the world so much that he gave his only Son, so that everyone who believes in him may not be lost but may have eternal life" (John 8.16).

In the same chapter, John reports the conversation between Jesus and the religious leader Nicodemus that has given the Church its apostolic directive. Though "religious," Nicodemus needed "new birth." Religion may be something tacked on; rebirth is a God-changed nature.

Help of Christians—pray for us.

DONALD CROWHURST

□ 6 □

Our Lady of Louvain—Belgium

Mary brought her Son to the Temple for the usual purification ceremonies because that was what was expected of any good mother in those days. And Mary was a good mother.

Every mother since has a positive and serious obligation to smother her children in love *and* care. Love comes naturally. Care takes more effort. Parents just can't be goofing off at local pubs all the time, or drinking their lunches with civic clubs. Children are far more precious than orchids. And they need a lot more care.

Parents owe their children an education in the profound mysteries of a good God and the works of His creation. Children should be taught about God right from the beginning. Any young people who contemplate being married without giving due thought to loving, caring for, or educating their children properly are sorely in need of prayer and proper instruction.

Queen of Angels—pray for us.

RICHARD MADDEN, O.C.D.

□ 7 □

Our Lady of Grace—Abbey of St. Sauve, Montreil-sur-Mer

Grant me the grace today, Lord, to accept Your word and to place my trust in You as Your Blessed Mother did. Let her be a model for me, as a person who was willing to devote her whole life to serving

Your Father. She accepted Your word and became Your Mother.

I am not faced with such an awesome responsibility, yet I often fail, and fail miserably, in even small things.

I am weak; I am afraid. I often find it hard to believe in You. Lord, help me today to remember the example of Your Mother, to know amid the confusion of everyday life that You are truly with me, that Your Kingdom is at hand.

Queen of Patriarchs—pray for us.

ROBERT MEEHAN

□ 8 □

Madonna of Miracles and Virtues—Rennes, France

Before displaying a precious gem, the jeweler seeks an attractive case so that the beauty of the stone might be better appreciated by those who view it.

Almighty God, working in a similar fashion, prepared a most perfect dwelling place for His Son through the Immaculate Conception of the Virgin Mary. As we give thanks to God for showing such favor to the Mother of the Redeemer, we also beg Him, for her sake, to give us, who have entered this world stained with original sin, the grace to preserve the purity conferred on us by baptism or restored by penance.

Our meditations today should also inspire us to remove from our lives any fault or sin that might mar the beauty of our souls in the sight of God. Surely our souls, which are the dwelling places of God, should be kept immaculate for such a guest.

Queen of Prophets—pray for us.

REV. MSGR. EDWARD W. O'MALLEY

□ 9 □

Our Lady of the Lily

The picture of "Mater Admirabilis," a fresco in the Sacred Heart Convent of Trinita dei Monti, Rome, represents our Lady, while still a child, in the Temple of Jerusalem, resting awhile from her daily toil of spinning. She has a wonderful air of modesty and recollection, external signs of her soul's interior communion with God. The modesty of eyes and demeanor shows that her soul is enjoying the presence of its Creator.

Impulsiveness of manner, the absence of self-restraint—such things are signs of an uncontrolled heart; of a soul set on things besides God. Whereas, if the interior sight is radiant from gazing on God, then bodily eyes, too, are filled with recollection.

A lily shown beside our Lady in the fresco suggests that we must aim at purity of life. Like the lily, our soul should stand out from its surroundings by its beauty. A soul stained with sin is like a flower decayed, full of evil odor.

Queen of Apostles—pray for us.

ALBERT POWER, S.J.

□ 10 □

Our Lady of the Dove—near Bologna, Italy

The purity of Mary is one of her virtues that has been extolled through the ages. "Virgin most pure," is how the litany puts it. Her purity led to an intimacy with Christ, and her intimacy with Christ led to her purity.

In a world punch-drunk with sex, purity gets a very bad press. Everywhere sex is exploited and purity spurned. Our "fast food" mentality wants the pleasure of sex and wants it now. No waiting. Many of our young people are becoming sexually active at a much earlier age. To speak of purity cuts diametrically across the trend of our times.

It takes courage today to face the ridicule and scurrility; to buck the social pressures without surrendering the ideal of purity. It is the virtue of the strong. We need a witness to that ideal. Mary is the witness. We need strength to witness to purity. Mary is the source of that strength.

Queen of Martyrs—pray for us.

ALBERT J. NIMETH, O.F.M.

FEBRUARY

☐ 11 ☐

Our Lady of Lourdes

The messages of the Virgin Mary to St. Bernadette at Lourdes stressed the need for penance and prayer. The Lady's messages were filled with her maternal expressions of love for all mankind.

From the early days of the Church, Mary has had a special place in the hearts of Jesus' followers. To the first apostles and disciples, she was friend and counselor; to early theologians, Mary's place in salvation history was clear—Mother of the Redeemer, special mediatrix, and spiritual mother of us all. We recognize and even take for granted Mary's concern and love for the Church today in our many prayers to her, in our many feasts and celebrations in her honor.

We can approach Mary in confidence with our needs, with a certainty that she will make our needs known to Jesus, her Son. *To Jesus through Mary.*

Queen of Confessors—pray for us.

LINUS MERZ, S.C.J.

☐ 12 ☐

Our Lady of Iveron—Moscow

Is it possible to sing a few lines of "The Lourdes Hymn" and not feel the thrill and enthusiasm of this Marian devotion? I can always envision the long lines of pilgrims, carrying candles, and singing mightily.

According to the old maxim, "Who sings well, prays twice," a Christian celebration without music would lack something almost essential. The resurgence of community singing in the restored liturgy is one of the healthier signs that it will survive.

Contemporary hymns accompanied by modern musical instruments are causing a new wind to blow through Christianity. "They will know we are Christians by our love, by our love" is a thrilling line to sing. So is "We will guard each man's dignity. . . ." Modern music is certainly a great help in the effort to make the Church relevant to a generation that really cares.

Queen of Virgins—pray for us.

REV. CHARLES DOLLEN

FEBRUARY

☐ 13 ☐

Our Lady of Hot Oven—Bourges, France

It is hard to picture our Lady doing anything except, perhaps, holding the Christ Child quietly or just standing there "like a statue." What is the place of our Lady in our lives? She was the first one to do the thing each one of us must do—she brought Christ into the world. That is the one major task we all have.

His life began in her when she bowed to the will of the Father and accepted the Holy Spirit. She said *yes*, and Christ began to grow in her. Wherever she went and whatever she did formed Christ in her so that one day she could give Him to others—to the world.

Lord, that is the goal of my life: to say *yes* to the Father so that the Holy Spirit, working in me, will enable me to bring Jesus to everyone I meet—"No longer me, but only Jesus!"

Queen of All Saints—pray for us.

THERESITA POLZIN

☐ 14 ☐

Our Lady of Pellovoisin—France

Mary is our mother and our model. Like a good and loving mother, she shows us the way. Our great goal in life is to be a little more like her; and the beautiful lesson she teaches us at every turn is to trust God. Her whole life was this.

So many times she did not understand; so much was mystery for her. Still she believed in the goodness of God, and that He, a gentle Father, would in His own way take care of us always.

Many times, Mary did not understand. At the Presentation of our Lord, the words of the old prophet were confusing to her. There were many other times too. Constantly she pondered all of these things, but always, even in the darkness, she trusted God. And she says to us: so should we.

Queen conceived without original sin—pray for us.

REV. RAWLEY MYERS

☐ 15 ☐

Notre Dame de Paris

In spite of the liturgical renewal and advance during the years following the Second Vatican Council, it is unlikely that the holy Rosary will cease to be an important part of Catholic piety and devotion.

In moments of numbed pain following a terrible accident, or in times of great sorrow, many "renewed" Catholics have found that the recitation of the Rosary still provides a certain value for them not easily obtained in other forms of devotion. It has often united a small group of strangers who somehow shared a common sense of pain or loss.

Yet devotion to our Lord's holy Mother must rest on joy. She reflects preeminently the glory of being close to her divine Son.

Queen assumed into heaven—pray for us.

REV. JOHN MC CARTHY

☐ 16 ☐

Madonna of the Thorn—near Chalon, France

Dear Jesus: quickly, after the soldier's spear has drawn water and blood from Your side, the crowd departs from Calvary. Then come Your friends to take Your body down from the cross. Gently, it is lowered and placed in the arms of Your Mother. As she held You as a baby, she holds You now; but her heart is breaking with grief.

As Mary received Your dead body from the cross, so I, my crucified Jesus, can receive Your living body as often as I will, in the sweet embrace of Holy Communion. But how often I have neglected this privilege in the past!

As I watch Mary tenderly receive Your dead body from the cross, I grieve for my neglect of Your body and blood in the past, and I promise to receive You often, daily if possible, in the blessed embrace of Holy Communion.

Queen of the most holy Rosary—pray for us.

DONALD F. MILLER, C.SS.R.

FEBRUARY

□ 17 □

Our Lady of Constantinople

The date October 7, 1571, may be ignored in the pages of world history, but it is a day to be remembered by all Christians. On that day, at Lepanto, the threat of the Turkish Empire to the civilization and culture of Christianity was ended.

How did the Christian forces win the battle? Chiefly through the recitation of the Rosary by Christian peoples everywhere. The situation was desperate. Victory for the enemy seemed almost certain. But Mary intervened in response to an appeal of Pope (St.) Pius V that all turn to Mary for assistance. The tide of battle changed miraculously, and Christianity was saved.

Are not circumstances almost similar today? The threat to world peace by the communist countries, especially Russia, is plainly visible. At Fatima, our Lady prescribed praying the Rosary daily as a weapon for peace. Christianity will be saved to the world through the Rosary!

Queen of Peace—pray for us.

MOST REV. JOHN J. CARBERRY

□ 18 □

Notre Dame de Laon — Church Erected by St. Remi

The Blessed Mother is the ladder by which Christians may ascend to heaven; she is in a sense the whole ground of their hope. Surely the Son cannot repulse her who gave Him birth.

Who could consider this, and not feel confidence in the Blessed Virgin Mary's protection and be wonderfully strengthened? Let us turn to our Mother with the love and confidence of a child.

St. Monica, by her persevering in prayer, obtained the complete conversion of her son, who became the great St. Augustine. How much more will the Blessed Virgin obtain God's grace for Christians, who are her children begotten by Calvary's agony! For their eternal welfare, she is more concerned even than St. Monica was for the salvation of her beloved son. — Joseph E. Snyder, *Salve Regina.*

Lamb of God, who take away the sins of the world—spare us, O Lord.

JOSEPH E. MANTON, C.SS.R.

□ 19 □

God's promise to David, "I will build *you* a house," turns the tables. All our good intentions, all our promises turn to nothing when God comes, for it is He who does everything. He is like the father who gives his son a quarter so the child can buy him a Christmas gift.

We are empty and helpless. Like Mary, we wait for the sun to rise, for God's grace to be revealed to us.

A Child is born bearing the names Wonderful, Counselor, Mighty God, Eternal Father, Prince of Peace. The glory of God, expected by the nations, is recognized by a few shepherds. To recognize Him, we too must be as receptive as cold darkness is to the rising sun, letting Christ flood us with His light and warmth.

O Rising Star, the brightness of God's eternal light, the sun of justice! Come, shed Your radiance upon us who languish in darkness and the shadow of death.

Lamb of God, who take away the sins of the world—graciously hear us, O Lord.

ANNE O'NEILL

□ 20 □

Mary's role in our public and private devotion is now so secure that we find it difficult to imagine a day when controversy raged about such a fundamental fact as her motherhood.

At the Council of Ephesus in 431, the assembled Fathers declared as Catholic faith the doctrine that the Blessed Virgin Mary was truly the Mother of Jesus. In 1931, Pope Pius XI celebrated the anniversary by issuing an encyclical in which he extolled Mary, with the Holy Family of Nazareth, as the foremost model of chaste married life and the religious education of youths. At the same time, he instituted the feast in honor of the divine Motherhood.

Whether married or single, each of us can appreciate the tremendous influence of family life, for individuals and for society. Aside from the moral implications, psychologists agree that the home affects a person's emotional health for his or her entire life. For our own families and for all others, let us pray to Mary, the Mother of God.

Lamb of God, who take away the sins of the world—have mercy on us.

REV. FRANCIS X. CANFIELD

□ 21 □

Our Lady of Good Haven—Dol, France

When she is giving a press conference or a speech, Mother Teresa's hands can be seen fingering her rosary. Her every act is a prayer. Devotion to our Lady is a hallmark of the Missionaries of Charity.

While instructing her Sisters, Mother Teresa says, "Let us ask our Lady to make our hearts meek and humble as her Son's. It is so very easy to be proud and harsh and selfish, so easy; but we have been created for greater things. How much we can learn from our Lady! She was so humble because she was all for God. She was full of grace. Tell our Lady to tell Jesus that they have no wine: that they need the wine of humility and meekness and kindness. She is sure to tell us to 'do whatever He tells you.' "

Pray for us, O holy Mother of God—that we may be made worthy of the promises of Christ.

ALICE COLLINS

□ 22 □

Our Lady of Help—Rennes, France

As Jesus approached the town of Naim, a funeral procession was coming out. A young man had died, the only son of a widow. The Gospel says that Jesus felt sorry for the mother and told the procession to stop. Then He said to the corpse, "Young man, I bid you get up." The young man arose, and Jesus gave him back to his mother.

This incident shows: a) The power of intercession: that God does good to one because of someone else. He raised the son because of the mother. b) That Jesus is moved by sensitive human feelings. He felt sorry for the mother. c) That Jesus has a special feeling for mothers, and, of course, for His own Mother especially.

It was because of His own Mother that Jesus worked His first miracle, at Cana. Go to Jesus through His Mother, and your prayers will be heard.

Let us pray. Grant, we beg You, O Lord God, that we Your servants may enjoy lasting health of mind and body, and by the glorious intercession of the Blessed Mary, ever virgin, be delivered from present sorrow and enter into the joy of eternal happiness.

VALERIAN SCHOTT, O.F.M.

☐ 23 ☐

Madonna of the Rocks—near Salamanca, Spain

No matter how hard they may try not to, many parents of large families have a favorite child. It may be the one who looks most like the father or the mother; or the one who was the firstborn, or the lastborn; or the one who cooperates best and shows the most affection and appreciation.

Parents don't want to be unfair, but they often find themselves favoring one child over others.

God, our Father, You are not unfair to the rest of us in showing such great favor to Mary. Of all Your earthly children, she cooperates with You most perfectly and loves You best. Let us rejoice in the favors You show her.

Through Christ our Lord. Amen.

GARY LAUENSTEIN, C.SS.R.

☐ 24 ☐

Cessation of Plague in Rome
Through Our Lady's Intercession— A.D. 591

Often we pray for something and do not get an answer, even after many years. Our Lord tells us to keep praying . . . to keep knocking at the door until someone answers. He tells us how much more readily does a father answer a son knocking at a door than a stranger!

God is our heavenly Father, and He wants to give us what is good. We have only to ask Him.

St. Anne, the mother of the Blessed Virgin Mary, prayed to become the mother of a child for many years before an angel appeared to her and her husband, Joachim, foretelling the birth of Mary. Anne's reward for her perseverance in prayer was to become the Grandmother of Christ the Savior.

We appreciate those things for which we work the hardest. Things won without a struggle hardly seem worthwhile. Sometimes it is a struggle to keep on praying. But we have assurance from Christ that God will answer if we do not stop.

Immaculate Heart of Mary—we offer ourselves to thee.

MARGARET HULA MALSAM

☐ 25 ☐

Our Lady of Victory—Constantinople

Thousands of people have found new spiritual richness in their lives when they turned to our most gracious Mother during a period when success or survival seemed impossible. Under the title of Our Lady of Victory, our Blessed Mother has granted special favors.

Pope Pius V, in 1571, designated October 7 as the feast of Our Lady of Victory. This feast day was instituted because of a victory granted Christian forces against the Turks. The vast Ottoman Empire, during that era, had intentions of conquering Rome, the center of Christendom. Since that victory by Christian forces, Our Lady of Victory has interceded many times and upheld Christian forces in minor and major wars. Confession, Holy Communion, and humble prayers have been the best methods of approaching our Lady.

Lord, have mercy—Christ, have mercy.

JOHN JULIUS FISHER

□ 26 □

Madonna of the Fields—Paris

Today is Mary's day. Say the Angelus. You've forgotten it? You never learned it? What a nice present to give to Mary, to begin it or renew it.

The Angelus is said three times each day, at six o'clock in the morning, twelve noon, and six o'clock in the evening.

"The Angel of the Lord declared unto Mary. *And she conceived by the Holy Spirit.* Hail, Mary . . .

"Behold the handmaid of the Lord. *Be it done unto me according to your word.* Hail, Mary . . .

"And the Word was made flesh. *And dwelt among us.* Hail, Mary . . .

"Let us pray. Pour forth, we beseech You, O Lord, Your grace into our hearts, that we, to whom the incarnation of Christ, your Son, was made known by the message of an angel, may, by His passion and cross, be brought to the glory of His resurrection. Through the same Christ our Lord. Amen."

Lord, have mercy—Christ, hear us.

TERRY MARTIN

□ 27 □

Our Lady of Lights—Lisbon

In the Book of Genesis, we read that God made two great lights: a greater light to rule the day, and a lesser light to rule the night. Cardinal Damien Philip Hugo says that "Christ is the greater light to rule the just, and Mary the lesser to rule the sinners—meaning that the sun is a figure of Jesus Christ, whose light is enjoyed by the just, who live in a clear day of divine grace; and that the moon is a figure of Mary, by whose means those who are in the night of sin are enlightened."

Since Mary is this auspicious luminary, and is so for the benefit of poor sinners, should anyone have been so unfortunate as to fall into the night of sin, what is he to do? Pope Innocent III replies, "Whoever is in the night of sin, let him cast his eyes on the moon, let him implore Mary." — St. Alphonsus de Liguori, *The Glories of Mary.*

Christ, graciously hear us.

MOST REV. ANDREW G. GRUTKA

FEBRUARY

□ 28 □

Our Lady, Refuge of Sinners—Quito, Ecuador

From childhood, we have been asking our Blessed Mother to pray for us at two very special times: now, right now; and at the hour of our death. In the "fourth promise," the Sacred Heart tells us that because of Mary's prayer, He will be "our secure refuge right now in life" and "at the moment of death."

His mercy will come to our aid to keep us in sanctifying grace or give grace back to us if we have lost it. And then when all the fears and horrors of our last illness and death rise up to challenge us, He will be at hand.

Within the open wound of His heart, according to the great preface of the Mass, saints will find a refuge of peace and rest, and sinners a haven of forgiveness and love. Both will be welcome, and both will be secure.

God the Father of heaven—have mercy on us.

EUGENE P. MURPHY, S.J.

□ 29 □

[Leap Year]

Once every four years, an extra day is given us to glorify God. At least we can think of it that way when we look at our calendars. This is that one day in four years. Why not make it memorable by the most perfect union we have ever had with our Divine Lord and Mary, His Mother?

If you knew the exact day on which you were to die, what would you do that day? St. Aloysius is supposed to have answered the question by saying he would keep on with what he was doing.

That is the perfect answer, *provided* what we are doing is for God's glory and out of love for Him. However, it *may* mean laying aside our petty interests and our concern for being better established on this earth, and devoting ourselves instead to the grand purpose of our existence. That purpose is to give glory to God by the more or less constant, loving thought for Him. Union is the goal of all love; union with God is life everlasting. But it starts here.

God the Son, Redeemer of the World—have mercy on us.

JOHN C. SELNER, S.S.

M A R C H

□ 1 □

In 1846, at the Sixth Provincial Council of Baltimore, our Lady was chosen as the patroness of the United States under this title: The Immaculate Conception. Her being thus honored was certainly a response to the devotional life of American Catholics.

There isn't a city in the United States that doesn't have a church (or churches) dedicated to the Blessed Virgin Mary. A listing of American churches whose names refer to Mary—the St. Marys, the Immaculate Conceptions, the Our Lady of Guadalupes—would be very lengthy.

Devotion to Mary always increases devotion to her Son. The last recorded words of Mary in the Gospels were spoken at the wedding feast at Cana: Whatever my Son tells you to do, do.

God the Holy Spirit—have mercy on us.

REV. CHARLES DOLLEN

◻ 2 ◻

Our Lady of Apparitions—Madrid

Mary's apparitions in the world are one form of her preaching of Christ. He is visible to us through her transparency; and He should be visible through all Christians as well. Jesus should be preached by us, as He is by her. Through this preaching of Christ, and not through reflections on human nature, fraternity, or human solidarity, the Church creates fraternity in the world.

By teaching the world that Christ's death is both a revelation of God's love for man and a manifestation of the depth of man's inhumanity and sin, the Church exercises its essential mission. In spite of all human attempts to ignore or impede it, the Church must ever remind us that what makes love among us possible is the fact that God loved us first in Christ, and that through His Spirit, Christ can become present in every person.

Holy Trinity, one God—have mercy on us.

ROMAN GINN, O.C.S.O.

◻ 3 ◻

Notre Dame de Longpont—Valois, France

Because Mary is both Virgin and Mother, she becomes the model of purity, not only for consecrated virgins but also for those whose love is sacramentalized in marriage. What makes her purity imitable by all, in varying degrees, is the fact that she kept her purity reserved for God's will. At first, she thought it would be reserved for serving God in the Temple. But by the visit of the angel, she learned it would be by bearing the Messiah. So the watchword of her purity was: "Be it done unto me according to thy word."

Purity is the guardian of love until God's will manifests itself. Mary's purity is a sign that each person is to keep his or her mystery sacred, until God's holy will determines the one to whom it is to be revealed. The preservation of personal innocence is not motivated by prudery, fear, or love of isolation, but by a passionate desire to preserve a secret until God gives the one to whom it can be whispered.

Immaculate Heart of Mary, most like the Sacred Heart of Jesus — pray for us.

G. JOSEPH GUSTAFSON, S.S.

☐ 4 ☐

Our Lady of Guard — Aragon, Spain

It was an interesting letter that Pope John XXIII wrote to the Archbishop of Turin: "Some time ago, I had occasion to say that little David stands always fearless and brave before Goliath the giant. He does not have powerful weapons, and the stones and slings which he holds would seem to be of little help to him. But he advances toward the enemy in the name of the Lord. The humble Pope of the Catholic Church also goes forward and carries with him only this modest and simple object of religious piety, the Rosary of Mary, and he pursues his task in the name of the Lord."

The Rosary may seem small and insignificant, but it is a most powerful instrument. Pope Leo XIII called it "a powerful means of renewing our courage, . . . a ready means to nurture one's faith and to keep one from ignorance of his religion, and to keep one from the danger of error."

Pope Pius XI urged the recitation of the Rosary against the evergrowing evils.

Immaculate Heart of Mary, whose soul was created without original sin—pray for us.

REV. MSGR. RALPH G. KUTZ

☐ 5 ☐

Our Lady of Good Aid—Nancy, Lorraine

Automobile travelers and workers in offices face almost constant irritations each day. Housewives and factory workers have their share of upsets as well. Each of us finds some humiliation in our path, no matter how talented we may be at forestalling mishaps. Yet we never have sufficient reason to grumble at inconvenience, for none of us loves God as well as we might. So why do we fret at the little trials He might send us?

The purpose of every trial is to enable us to love Him better, to withdraw just a bit more from the allurements of the world that knows Him not.

Our Blessed Mother lived every day of her life perfectly. God was delighted with her. Yet He did not spare her many fearful trials. Could you have borne the cross of knowing that you had lost Jesus for three days? Could you have stood watching while He writhed in agony on His own cross? If Mary was sent these trials to intensify her love for God, then let us welcome our own trials with open arms, as the saints have done.

Immaculate Heart of Mary, who said to God's messenger, "Be it done to me according to your word"—pray for us.

REV. DONALD F. X. CONNOLLY

□ 6 □

Our Lady of Nazareth—Pierre-Noire, Portugal

Twice in his Gospel—after the shepherds "paid their respects" to the newborn Jesus and again after Mary and Joseph found Him at the age of twelve in the Temple—St. Luke noted that "Mary treasured all these things and reflected on them in her heart." It was his way of saying that she was a meditative person.

We have to be meditative persons too, and for the same reason Mary was: to be able to discern and to understand, to the extent that we can, the working out of God's plan in our lives and times.

Thinking Mary's thoughts about her Son and His works is the theme of the type of meditation that makes the Rosary a living experience rather than a difficult or sterile exercise of memory.

Immaculate Heart of Mary, who always remained sinless—pray for us.

FELICIAN A. FOY, O.F.M.

□ 7 □

Madonna of the Star—Villa-Vicoiza, Portugal

The morning star is the herald of the dawning day, and the Virgin Mary is depicted as the herald of redemption. The Old Testament has proclaimed her the Virgin who was to conceive and bear a Son who would be the Savior of all.

For many reasons, it is appropriate that we call her the Morning Star. When Holy Mary gave birth to Jesus, she brought into the world the light that would end the groping through many years of darkness and confusion.

Christians who pray and honor Mary, the Morning Star, open beautiful new vistas. Glimpses have been revealed to some—of the shining eternal horizon that can be obtained when we imitate her Son.

Immaculate Heart of Mary, to whom the Angel Gabriel first announced the Good News—pray for us.

JOHN JULIUS FISHER

□ 8 □

Our Lady of Virtues—Lisbon

God honored Mary as no other person has been honored. From all generations, from all time, He chose her to be the Mother of His only-begotten Son.

From the first moment of her being, she was filled with divine life. Through her was to come the One who would redeem the world, who would return divine life to mankind. And God, that she might be a pure channel for the Incarnation, gave to her the fruits of the redemption that was to come.

That good and saintly woman, Miss Caryll Houselander, wrote: "It is our Lady—and no other saint—whom we can really imitate. . . . Each saint has his special work; one person's work. But our Lady had to include in her vocation, in her life's work, the essential thing that was to be hidden in every other vocation, in every life. She is not only human, she is humanity. The one thing that she did and does is the one thing we all have to do, namely, to bear Christ into the world. Christ must be born from every soul, formed in every life."

Immaculate Heart of Mary, who awaited the Savior with the greatest love—pray for us.

DALE FRANCIS

□ 9 □

Foundation of Savigny in Normandy in Honor of Our Lady—1112

It is the little things that really count. Many of the saints never did extraordinary things; they just accepted the little crosses that came their way. They lived an ordinary life in an extraordinary way!

MARCH

Mary is mentioned only a few times in Scripture, yet her role in history is incalculable. Christ spent the first thirty years of His life living simply, in obedience to Mary and Joseph.

We must offer up our day-to-day sacrifices as little crosses to God and perform our daily tasks with a cheerful, willing spirit. We must seek our "stardom" by accepting our roles, however insignificant they may seem, and by offering our works up for the honor and glory of God.

Immaculate Heart of Mary, within whom we see the beginning of the Church—pray for us.

MARGARET HULA MALSAM

□ 10 □

Madonna of the Vine—near Viterbo, Tuscany

Certain expressions from the Gospels have a way of clinging to our memories. Take "the reed shaken by the wind." Surely John the Baptist was no such willy-nilly, shiftless, fickle reed. He was strong, powerful, undaunted in his mission of announcing the coming of Christ.

Mary, the Mother of God, can well be compared to a reed, though not the kind shaken by the wind. She was rather a firm, graceful reed that God himself plucked out of the garden of earth. He then hollowed out this reed and filled it with all the grace He could lavish on a creature. In His hands, this reed we call Mary became the instrument God used to fill the world with His love song.

God wants all of us to become His reeds. Of course, He knows and we know that we will never become so perfect a reed as the Mother of His Son. But He does expect that we will become so docile and humble that He will be able to use us too as His instruments for filling the world with His love song.

Immaculate Heart of Mary, who remained always a virgin in giving us Jesus—pray for us.

REV. VINCENT A. YZERMANS

MARCH

□ 11 □

Madonna of Forests—Porto, Portugal

"O Mary, guide us, give us light in the dark night; show us the way as we wander in this bleak wilderness. Take us to your Son and our heavenly home."

Mary will help us; she always does. As St. Bernard wrote in the beautiful prayer *Memorare*: "Remember, O most gracious Virgin Mary, that never was it known that anyone who fled to thy protection . . . was left unaided."

She was the nurse of Jesus in His helpless infancy, and the teacher of His youth in their happy home at Nazareth. How many times she held Him as a babe in her arms and hugged Him close. How many times she brushed away a tear when, as a little boy, He fell or hurt Himself. How then can He refuse her anything?

Immaculate Heart of Mary, Queen of Peace, who gave us the Prince of Peace—pray for us.

REV. RAWLEY MYERS

□ 12 □

Our Lady of Miracles

Cardinal Newman, an Anglican who became a Catholic, once wrote: "No one has access to the Almighty as His Mother has; none has merit such as hers. Her Son will deny her nothing that she asks and herein lies her power. While she defends the Church, neither height nor depth, neither men nor evil spirits, neither great monarchs nor craft of man, nor popular violence can avail to harm us; for human life is short, but Mary reigns above, a Queen forever."

We often go to Jesus through Mary. We believe that just as she interceded at the wedding feast at Cana, so now she can speak to her Son on our behalf. "To Jesus through Mary" indicates that while we call upon Mary, Christ is always our goal.

One reason for honoring the Virgin Mary is that she is, indeed, the Mother of our Lord; but the best reason, experience shows, is that "it works."

Immaculate Heart of Mary, who conceived Jesus in your heart before conceiving Him in your womb—pray for us.

JOHN M. MARTIN, M.M.

MARCH

☐ 13 ☐

Our Lady of the Empires—Rome

Mary is queen of heaven; and it is with a warranted filial pride that we lay praise to her queenship. That we recognize her queenship is entirely consistent with the excellence of her whole being, derived principally from her motherhood of Him who is king by right, by inheritance, and by conquest of Satan.

She reigns over the Church, which acknowledges and extols her gentle rule and seeks her as a safe refuge in the calamities of our day. She reigns over the minds of men that they may seek only what is true; over their wills that they may follow only what is good; over their hearts that they may love only what she loves.

Through our efforts she will reign in the streets and squares, in the cities and the villages, in the valleys and on the mountains. Through the example of our love for Mary, we can lead all people to understand that hers is a reign of mercy in which every petition is heard, every sorrow comforted, every infirmity healed.

Immaculate Heart of Mary, who first adored the newborn Savior—pray for us.

G. JOSEPH GUSTAFSON, S.S.

☐ 14 ☐

Our Lady of Kostrama—Russia

A personal visit from the Mother of God would be a wonderful privilege. Yet each of us can visit with her every day through Mary's special prayer, the Rosary.

The communist symbol of hammer and sickle continues to represent torture for the innocent and enslaved. The Rosary does not hurt; it heals. Its material is just a few beads and a small piece of wood. Its material strength is insignificant compared with the mighty arms of the godless. Yet the strongest nations have never been able to conquer the cross and prayer.

Every time we kneel to pray the Rosary, we are doing the one thing that the communists would not dare to do; for if they knelt in prayer, the hammer and sickle would fall from every communist flag in the world. . . . Communists would be forced to hear the words of our Lord, "A new commandment I give unto you, that you love one another."

Immaculate Heart of Mary, Mother of love in the holy family at Nazareth—pray for us.

REV. MSGR. HARRY J. WELP

□ 15 □

Miraculous Deliverance of Chartres by Our Lady in A.D. 911

Let us go to Mary and ask her protection in our world filled with tension and growing frustrations. Let us ask our Mother's help to resist temptations against chastity, a virtue constantly being attacked.

There are places where the chaste are scorned because they dare to be different, because they yearn to obey God's laws. Those who profess chastity need Mary's help. Mary can inspire those who have pledged to observe the virtue of chastity. She *can* help, for, after Christ, Mary is our most powerful intercessor in heaven. Whatever Mary asks, Christ gives. Let us go to Mary.

Immaculate Heart of Mary, whose immaculate soul and virginal body were taken into heaven—pray for us.

MARIE LAYNE

□ 16 □

Our Lady of the Fountain—Constantinople

"We see the Blessed Virgin as a lamp of living light shining upon those in darkness; she enkindles an unearthly light to lead all unto divine knowledge; she, the Radiance that enlightens the mind, is praised by our cry."

This eloquent outburst from the Akathistos Hymn is almost as ancient as Christianity itself, for Christians have always seen that Mary had a special role in the "economy" of salvation. She was truly the Mother of God, but there is more than that in her mission to us. Through her, God became a man; but she was not a passive instrument. Her whole being bent to His intentions. Her every human faculty and every divine gift were dedicated to this mighty task. And thus she became the model of all who seek God. For she was a conscious, living instrument of God's will.

Immaculate Heart of Mary, Mother of God and Mother of us all—pray for us.

REV. CLIFFORD STEVENS

□ 17 □

Institution of Our Lady's Office—1095

Our Lady is the queen and mother of contemplatives. Not only was Mary closer to our Lord than anyone else; we are also distinctly told that she reflected deeply—meditated, that is—on what He said and did. Thus we read in St. Luke's second chapter: "But Mary treasured up all these sayings, and reflected on them in her heart." Again, "The father and mother of the Child were still wondering over all that was said of him." Yet again, "His mother kept in her heart the memory of all this."

Virgin most reflective, Virgin most prayerful, Virgin most contemplative: these are titles that might justly be included in a private litany to our Lady. And surely this good Mother, whose contemplation of the Light of the World was so deep and uninterrupted, will eagerly assist us in our honest efforts to practice a prayer that will be far more than the repetition of pious formulas.

Immaculate Heart of Mary, Queen of guardian angels—pray for us.

VINCENT P. MC CORRY, S.J.

□ 18 □

Our Lady of Loreto;
St. Joseph, Spouse of Our Lady

Since the intercession of St. Joseph is so needed in these trying times, we can suitably and profitably turn our thoughts to him. Pope Pius XI said of St. Joseph, "As the chosen spouse of the Virgin Mother of God, he was a participant in her dignity by reason of their conjugal union; Christ the Son of God wished him to be His guardian and to be thought His father as well; he was head of the divine household on earth with, as it were, fatherly authority; he has the Church dedicated to his loyalty and protection. Such a person possesses so surpassing a dignity that no honor exists that should not be paid to him.''

Thus are listed St. Joseph's titles to our deep reverence and special regard. He was chosen for a unique relationship to the Redeemer and the Co-Redemptrix. Just as they were under his care, so is the Church; and so is each member of the Church.

Immaculate Heart of Mary, Queen of all angels and saints—pray for us.

REV. MSGR. JOHN S. KENNEDY

□ 19 □

Our Lady of Fair—Norgent-sur-Seine; Feast of St. Joseph

The Church honors St. Joseph as worker and husband. Joseph must have been a remarkable man indeed, to be chosen first among men as the foster father and teacher of the boy Jesus.

In America today, as unemployment varies and the cost of living edges up and up, the husband-fathers are prey to tensions and concerns that unnerve and worry. More than ever, they need the basic virtue that steadied the hand and heart of St. Joseph. That virtue is confidence in God. Joseph trusted in God when he married the Virgin Mary, when he traveled with her to Bethlehem, fled with her and the infant Jesus to Egypt, and finally settled down with them to long hard years in Nazareth. God grant that all fathers and families be sustained in adversity by a strong, resolute confidence in Him.

Immaculate Heart of Mary, who kept the word of God in your heart—pray for us.

EDWIN R. MC DEVITT, M.M.

□ 20 □

Our Lady of Calevoirt—Uckelen, Belgium

Christ our Savior praised His Mother, Mary, not merely because she was His Mother physically, but because she had all the interior virtues and, above all, faith—to hear God's word and to keep and practice it.

Mary is always our model in every way, but sometimes our idea of her is too vague to imitate. Today let us see if we depend too much on the externals of our faith—like saying certain prayers, going to church, having holy statues and pictures in our homes. These things are good, but of themselves profit nothing without inner faith, prayer, and Christian charity. Above all, we must serve Christ daily by being of service to our neighbor.

Immaculate Heart of Mary, whose soul Simeon said a sword would pierce—pray for us.

SISTER M. CHARLES BORROMEO, C.S.C.

☐ 21 ☐

Our Lady of Bruges—Flanders

Unlike so many other creatures, Mary does not separate us from God. On the contrary, she draws and leads us to God. As one author puts it, "The devotion and love of the Son increases with that which men bear the mother, because the mother, being most faithful to the Son, draws and conducts to Him all who approach her, and endeavors to reconcile and unite them more closely to God."

Therefore, the more we love Mary, the more we shall love God. There is no shorter, easier, or safer path to attain to the perfect love of God than the tender and sincere love of Mary. But this love of Mary must be strong, persevering, tender, and fervent.

The will of God expressed in the commandment "Honor thy father and thy mother" obliges us to love her who is our Mother in the supernatural order.

Immaculate Heart of Mary, praying with the Apostles for the Church—pray for us.

SEBASTIAN V. RAMGE, O.C.D.

☐ 22 ☐

Notre Dame de Cîteaux

Of all the lessons of this feast, we should not overlook Mary's happiness because of her sinlessness, her fullness of grace, her union with God. It is difficult for all but the saints—and they had their struggles—to imagine a state of happiness not somehow related to our life in this world, our human loves and satisfactions, our peace, security, and material possessions.

St. Teresa used to say: "God alone suffices." If we had the world and God we would have no more than if we had God alone. How deeply do we appreciate this truth?

The major task of faith is to persuade us that happiness, sole and supreme, can be found in holiness, in loving union with God, in freedom from sin and all attachment to sin, in the renunciation even of the natural ties that bind us to the earth, though not sinful in themselves. Mary's whole life is in her Magnificat; and it is above all a hymn of pure joy.

Immaculate Heart of Mary, desiring sacrifices for the conversion of sinners—pray for us.

MOST. REV. LEO A. PURSLEY

□ 23 □

Our Lady of Victory

Because of her singular role, Mary admits of no classification. Rather, she stands superior to all categories as Queen—Queen of Apostles, Martyrs, Confessors, Virgins . . . as we pray in her Litany.

Holy Mary, Virgin, Mother of God, plead our cause. These few words proclaim all of Mary's greatness. We cite with them her personal sanctity; her special predilection as virgin and mother, the basic reason for all her other graces; her intercessory power, from which stems the boundless trust that clients place in the "Help of Christians."

Immaculate Heart of Mary, comfort to souls at the hour of death — pray for us.

REV. MSGR. DAVID P. SPELGATTI

□ 24 □

Vigil of the Annunciation

In one of his *Missus Est* homilies, St. Bernard gives us a heaven's-eye view of the Annunciation. He pictures the whole court of heaven watching as Gabriel utters that fateful *Ave!* All wait for Mary's answer.

MARCH

God willed that the Word would be made flesh through Mary. Suppose she had said "No," instead of "Behold the slave-girl of the Lord; be it done as you have explained it." The supposition is simply unthinkable. As one spiritual writer explains it, Mary had conceived Christ in her soul by faith, hope, and love, long before she received Him in her womb.

Any woman could have performed that latter service. Mary is a heroic model of the great theological virtues—the first Christian.

Immaculate Heart of Mary, at whose request Jesus turned water into wine—pray for us.

REV. CHARLES DOLLEN

□ 25 □

Annunciation of the Lord

Today's feast really celebrates two events: God's predilection of Mary to be His Mother, and the revelation of the mystery of the Incarnation in Gabriel's message to Mary.

The court of heaven must have held its breath momentarily as it waited for Mary's response. Her fiat—"Let it be done to me as you say"—has been a model through all ages of faith-filled acceptance of God's will in one's regard. No wonder Luke tells us: "Mary treasured all these things and reflected on them in her heart." Although she was told that the holy offspring to be born would be called the Son of God, subsequent events in her life required prayerful reflection and deep faith for her to live out her role in human salvation. No blueprint was given to her; nor has one been given to each of us.

Let us pray for grace to imitate Mary's faith, and recall the mysteries of this feast by a daily recitation of the Angelus.

Immaculate Heart of Mary, offering Jesus in sacrifice on Mount Calvary—pray for us.

SISTER LORRAINE DENNEHY, C.S.J.

☐ 26 ☐

Our Lady of Soissons—France

Workmen building the great cathedrals in honor of Mary, in the ages of faith, were motivated in large measure by their devotion to her. If a pinnacle, buttress, mosaic, or mural enhanced the structure and added to the honor of the Blessed Mother, it was added without question. Even unseen parts were painted or sculptured with meticulous care. The only thing that mattered was: Will it be pleasing to Mary?

If we are motivated to live our lives in a way that is always pleasing to Mary, we can be sure our lives will also be pleasing to God. In the final analysis, this is all that counts. With this in mind, we do well to take stock of ourselves. This criterion may prompt us to rearrange our priorities, to live the motto *Through Mary to Jesus.* Christ then becomes the primary objective of our endeavors. And that is the right order of things.

Immaculate Heart of Mary, and our Lady of the Most Holy Eucharist — pray for us.

ALBERT J. NIMETH, O.F.M.

☐ 27 ☐

*Apparition of Our Lord to Our Lady
after His Resurrection*

"If any one would tell you the shortest, surest way to all happiness and all perfection," William Law wrote, "he must tell you to make it a rule to yourself to thank and praise God for everything that happens to you." The Mother of Sorrows kept this rule.

Have you ever pictured Mary in the home St. John provided after Jesus entrusted her to his care? Did she sometimes sit on a low stool talking with Luke? Did his gentle, healing hands enclose hers as he encouraged her to share memories for the Gospel he was to write? Was some of her sorrow eased by confiding to a sympathetic physician? Did she smile telling of the infant, the growing boy, the teenaged carpenterson who was subject to His parents?

MARCH

Little wonder that we go to the Blessed Lady so confidently with our petitions, sure of the comfort of her mothering arms.

Immaculate Heart of Mary, teacher of us in the way of God—pray for us.

MARION EGAN

□ 28 □

Our Lady of Castel Bruedo

"Who is she that cometh forth as the morning rising: fair as the moon; bright as the sun; terrible as an army in battle array?" Jesus took His Mother up to heaven body and soul because Mary was without sin—and ever a Virgin—and the Mother of God.

When Jesus ascended into heaven, Mary remained on earth "in exile" for some years afterward. Very little is found in Holy Scripture about Mary. She was "the Woman wrapped in silence. . . . All the glory of the King's daughter is within."

Mary was "full of grace" from the first moment of her conception and yet had gone on increasing in grace and love every moment of her life. "Pentecost was Mary's special Bethlehem, the new Epiphany, in which as Mother standing by the Crib of the Mystic Christ, she makes Him known once again to other shepherds and other kings" (Fulton J. Sheen).

Mary is the cause of our joy, and the Gate of Heaven for all the saints.

Immaculate Heart of Mary, living example of the love of humility—pray for us.

MOST REV. REMBERT KOWALSKI, O.F.M. (China)

□ 29 □

Apparition of Our Lady to St. Bonet

Next to the Lord's Prayer, the Hail Mary is the prayer most frequently recited each day. The first part of it contains the words of the Archangel Gabriel to Mary at the Annunciation, and then the words of Elizabeth to Mary at the time of Mary's visit to her (Luke 1.28, 42). The second part, a petition, reminds us that we pray within the community of faith, live within it, and rely on the prayers of others.

Mention of the Hail Mary brings to mind the Rosary of the Blessed Mother. This popular form of prayer combines meditation on the mysteries of faith with the recitation of vocal prayers, mainly the Hail Mary. Those who would reject the Rosary on the ground that it is repetitious and ill-suited to sophisticated moderns could well heed the words of Pope Pius XII: "We do not hesitate to affirm publicly that we put great confidence in the Holy Rosary for the healing of evils which afflict our times." The Rosary is the prayer for all seasons, for all people, for all needs.

Immaculate Heart of Mary, perfect model of adoring the Father through Christ in the Spirit—pray for us.

THOMAS M. BREW, S.J.

□ 30 □

Our Lady of Boulogne-sur-Mer

We speak often about listening, about lending an ear to the words that God so gently speaks, about being attentive to the Father's voice. Can any better example be found than in the total listening of the Mother of Jesus?

"Hail Mary," said the angel, and Mary listened with awesome faith and hope to hear that she, indeed, was filled with grace. Within her was to reside the fulfillment of all the promises that had been given to man. Her child was to be a child for all the world, the one in whom all good things would be accomplished. Throughout her life, Mary listened. Her distress when her Son was lost in Jerusalem; the heartache of witnessing her Son's crucifixion; her awesome acceptance of her purpose in life—all these are examples of Mary's ability to listen.

We should strive to listen as Mary did. The Lord still speaks to His earth. Still His voice encircles us; and we must listen. In the rain and dew, the cold and chill, the Lord speaks to His children.

Immaculate Heart of Mary, Mother of the Church and spouse of the Holy Spirit—pray for us.

T. TIMOTHY DELANEY

MARCH

☐ 31 ☐

Our Lady of the Holy Cross—Jerusalem

Never loved son his mother as Jesus loved Mary. Never loved mother her son as this Queen of Sorrows loved the Man of Sorrows. When our Lord permitted His Mother to suffer with Him at the foot of the cross, He added, beyond question, a grief to His own tender heart infinitely beyond our poor power of understanding. We can only look at it dumbly, like those who pass by the way, knowing there could be no sorrow like unto this.

Mary's sorrow was matched also by her magnificent courage. What a disservice to her are those sentimental pictures of a swooning Virgin, making her look for all the world like a Hollywood actress!

When Mary turned away from the foot of the cross, at the ninth hour, when all was over, she knew that our redemption had been wrought. The price had been fearful; but if it were all to do over again, she would not hesitate.

Immaculate Heart of Mary, Mother of Christ and our Mother in the Communion of Saints — pray for us.

MOST REV. ROBERT J. DWYER

APRIL

□ 1 □

Our Lady of Tears

There is a statue—at a church in England—of a Madonna who once held the Child but now holds nothing. At the Reformation, the image of the child was removed from the arms of the mother in an effort to show that devotion to Mary was ended. The reformers couldn't keep the little statue of Christ without the statue of the mother to hold it, so they destroyed the small one.

Those who begin by trying to destroy our love of Mary often wind up by denying her Son also. If Jesus is God, then His Mother is the greatest of humans. If He is our brother, then Mary is our mother—and we cannot ignore her.

Evening Masses are now taking the place of some parish devotions; but I'm sure Mary doesn't mind. She is still leading us to the feet of her Son.

Immaculate Heart of Mary, crowned as Queen in heaven by the Most Blessed Trinity—pray for us.

REV. MSGR. MAURICE COONEY

□ 2 □

Visitation of Our Lady at York—1263-1389

Sacred Scripture reveals little about Mary, but the few glimpses it does disclose wonderfully spotlight her humanness. The visit to Elizabeth, for example, provides us with a beautiful insight into her thoughtfulness toward others.

Mary saw someone in need, she saw the opportunity to help; she came to that person's assistance. It was as simple—and as difficult—as that. The episode itself is so ordinary and human that it puts her within reach of each of us. It is not what she did that was so important, but the love that motivated her action.

In a sense, we can make the blind beggar's plea ours: "Lord, that I may see." There are any number of opportunities for us to show our love for God and neighbor by acts of thoughtfulness. We have only to be alert and receptive to them. . .then generous enough to give ourselves in the performance of them.

Immaculate Heart of Mary, praying for our salvation—pray for us.

WILLIAM J. NEIDHART, C.S.C.

□ 3 □

Apparition of Our Lord to His Mother and the Apostles
after the Resurrection

The Apostles were holy men working under the direction of their Master. They were chosen to assist in establishing a spiritual kingdom, just as Mary had been chosen to be the Mother of their Master.

Mary, through her involvement with Jesus, became the Queen of the Apostles. Our world today needs many men and women to carry on the good work. Through Holy Mary's help, this sublime purpose will finally be fulfilled.

Mary's part in our salvation has grown throughout the years. She is definitely the Queen of all seekers of grace, peace, and love. She can help us in obtaining an increase of apostolic vocations.

Immaculate Heart of Mary, full of grace and Mother of grace—pray for us.

JOHN JULIUS FISHER

APRIL

□ 4 □

Our Lady of Grace—Normandy

The Angel Gabriel told Mary that she was "full of grace," the Lord lived with her. We too are called to this same fullness of life by Jesus, who told us to "be perfect as my heavenly Father is perfect." Is it possible that we tend to excuse ourselves from imitating Mary's life of total loving response to our Father because we feel that somehow it was easier for her to do the Lord's will? She was conceived without sin; we weren't. Yet, wasn't Adam too created without sin? Was it any harder for him to fall?

Through our baptism and reception of the other sacraments, the Lord is continually with us too. The main difference between each of us and Mary is that she constantly did anything our Father asked, never doubting that it was for her benefit, or that He could help her.

Immaculate Heart of Mary, desiring to give grace to children who ask—pray for us.

C. RUSSELL DITZEL

□ 5 □

Apparition of Our Lady to Pope Honorius IV
to Confirm the Order of Our Lady of Mount Carmel

The motherhouse of the Carmelite Order stood on the top of Mount Carmel, on the coast of Palestine. In 1251, the Blessed Virgin Mary appeared there to Simon Stock, General of the Order, and gave him the scapular, with the promise that anyone dying while wearing it would be saved. She asked him also to have the Carmelites dedicate themselves to her service and to wearing the scapular.

Even Mary as Queen of Heaven never speaks for herself only. She speaks for her Son, our Lord: Therefore, in her later appearances at Guadalupe, Lourdes, Fatima, and elsewhere, she has been acting as God's favored messenger to us. We ask her to intercede for us with Jesus. No intercession by all the other saints is as powerful.

We do well to heed what she tells us. She heals at Lourdes. At Fatima, in 1917, she asked us to pray fervently to her Son, lest communism's errors contaminate the whole world. We can see we have not prayed enough.

Immaculate Heart of Mary, ever ready to hear the prayers of children—pray for us.

PAUL KOCHER

□ 6 □

Our Lady of the Conception—Douai, France

On this glorious feast of Mary, we reflect on Mary's sinlessness and obedience. We hear her beautiful response to the angel: "Behold the handmaid of the Lord. Be it done to me according to your word." Not knowing exactly what God wanted of her as His Mother, she willingly said yes to all. Mary as our Mother, and as Mother of the Church, gives us the perfect example of obedience.

Mary, from her earliest years, responded completely and totally to the call of God. She submitted to what she did not fully understand, for God's love and goodness in her radiated beyond her understanding. The angel did not completely answer her question but addressed her faith in God's power and goodness.

Mary is a truly loving Mother who watches over all her children on earth, caring for them and interceding to her Son for their needs. Let us renew today our personal devotion to her.

Immaculate Heart of Mary, wounded in love by the sins of men—pray for us.

SISTER CAROL ANN KENZ, C.S.J.

□ 7 □

Our Lady of the Forsaken—Valencia, Spain

We must thank God for past and present humiliations, calumnies, unkind interpretations of our words, deeds, omissions, or intentions, the detractions we have suffered from, and everything that has ever happened to mortify our self-love.

If we consider the true interests of our soul, it is a real blessing to be humbled and kept down, not only because it helps us to advance in the way of perfection, but also because of the innumerable opportunities it gives us of glorifying God and acquiring merit, and of being so much higher in heaven. Humility must be a law of the world of grace, because we find it in Mary, in the Saints, and, in the faintest, most nearly indistinguishable way, in ourselves. Perhaps it is something inseparable from God. — F.W. Faber, *The Foot of the Cross.*

Immaculate Heart of Mary, hope and comfort for merciful forgiveness—pray for us.

G. JOSEPH GUSTAFSON, S.S.

□ 8 □

Feast of the Miracles of Our Lady—Cambron, Belgium

On the cross, Jesus said to His Mother, "Woman, there is your son," and to St. John, "There is your Mother," thus bequeathing His own Mother to all of us represented by John at that hour of death.

As always, Mary took those words to heart. She cares for us as her adopted children. Repeatedly through the ages, she has come back to the world to direct us to Jesus. She taught St. Dominic the Rosary in Spain; she gave Juan Diego her picture and asked for a church in Mexico; she announced her Immaculate Conception at Lourdes, France; she called for prayer and penance at Fatima, Portugal, in our own day. Like a good mother, she is concerned about our salvation, using her power of intercession to obtain for us—if we cooperate—a union with her Son in our daily lives so that her adopted children may someday share the Kingdom of her Son by birth.

Immaculate Heart of Mary, perfect model of reparation—pray for us.

THERESITA POLZIN

□ 9 □

Our Lady of Myans — Chambrey, Savoy

Mary is so kind and courteous that she is ever with us. She keeps us company in solitude; accompanies us on our journeys; counsels us in doubt; consoles us in affliction; assists us in sickness; defends us from our enemies, visible and invisible. She also encourages us in fear and protects us from the anger and vengeance of God. If we call her, she answers promptly; if we salute her, she courteously returns the salutation; if we praise her, she kindly thanks us; if we do her any service, she abundantly reimburses us; if we show her faith and love, she gives us the most tender proofs of her affection. St. Catherine of Siena said that Mary is a most sweet bait that God has prepared to catch the hearts of men.

Immaculate Heart of Mary, triumph of all who believe in God's word—pray for us.

SEBASTIAN V. RAMGE, O.C.D.

□ 10 □

Our Lady of Laval—Viverais, France

Unless we know who Jesus was, how attractive, how holy, how gentle, how magnetic, how kindly, how majestic—and at the same time divine—we cannot appreciate how Mary's heart was a Chapel of Sorrows that black Good Friday afternoon. She heard those blood-stained lips murmur the trembling word "Mother"—but even as she looked up, she saw His glazed eyes close, His body stiffen—and Jesus, her Son, was dead. The life of Jesus, the light of her life, was blown out like a candle. And she was alone in the dark.

When trouble throws the dark shadow of its cross upon our bright path, never think that nobody ever endured what we endure. The Mother of God majored in sorrow. Nobody ever lost as much as Mary, because there was no Treasure like Jesus.

Pray for us, O holy Mother of God. . .

JOSEPH E. MANTON, C.SS.R.

□ 11 □

Madonna of Montserrat

Mary shines forth on earth as the Mother of Jesus, "as a sign of sure hope and solace for the Pilgrim People of God," the Second Vatican Council declared. In the bodily and spiritual glory she possesses in heaven, the Mother of Jesus continues in this present world as the image and first flowering of the Church, they also said.

Mary is our special ambassador. We ask her to intercede for us. As spouse of the Holy Spirit, who overshadowed her so she could be the Mother of Christ, Mary is linked in a special way to God. Yet she was fully human — like ourselves in every way except that she was miraculously preserved from any sin.

We have a heavenly Father who loves us, but we also have a Mother in heaven who watches after us with a truly motherly love. Her sinless Immaculate Heart is brimming with love for us.

That we may be made worthy of the promises of Christ.

MARGARET HULA MALSAM

□ 12 □

Our Lady of Charity—near Toulouse, France

It is hard to believe that we can take so lightly the fact that God has chosen us to receive favors. I suppose it is because not many of us are the type of person who is in the right place at the right time to be chosen for favors. Sounds too good to be true. Usually we stumble into everything.

Nevertheless, here we are, like Mary, right where we are, doing routine, everyday things—and we've been chosen! Unfortunately, we don't have that humble unreserved submission that Mary had. God knows that. God knows how hard it is for us to change our plans and give up doing something we want to do to serve others. He knows and still He asks us to do it. Each day, let us make a sacrifice; do something special for someone, for love of God. Let us be aware that we have been chosen, and ask Mary to help us show our gratitude.

Let us pray—O sorrowful and Immaculate Heart of Mary, . . .

MUJANA DARIAN

□ 13 □

Our Lady's Apparition to Blessed Jane of Mantua

Just as the Son of God once took upon Himself human nature from the womb of Mary, overshadowed by the Holy Spirit, so now He takes a new Body from the womb of humanity, overshadowed by the same Holy Spirit. Just as He once taught, governed, and sanctified through human nature, so now He continues to teach, to govern, and to sanctify through other human nature which makes His Body.

APRIL

The Mystical Body of Christ, therefore, no more stands between Christ and me, than His Physical Body stood between Magdalen and His forgiveness, or His hand stood between the little children and His blessing; but it was through His human body that He came to men in His individual life. It is through His Mystical Body that He comes to us in His Mystical Corporate Life.

I consider that the greatest blessing Almighty God has given to me is to be united with His Body. I thank Thee, O Christ, that I am a member of Thy Body! What a joy to be a Catholic!

Mother and model of the Church, . . .

MOST REV. FULTON J. SHEEN

□ 14 □

Our Lady's Apparition to St. Ludvina

Mary gave God ears to delight in the sounds of nature, to thrill to the song of the birds, and to revel in the harmony of the spheres. These are the ears that listened to the tales of the hurt and the wounded, that waited to hear and eagerly responded to pleas for mercy and forgiveness, that welcomed the expressions of penitence, faith, and love. Mary gave God ears that heard the jeers and blasphemies of the ungrateful people who shouted, "Crucify him!"

If today God is to listen to the cries for help or attend to the stories of the nervous and the neurotic, we have to give Him our ears. We have to allow Him to listen through us. Nobody listens to anyone any more. The lonely, the aged, the imprisoned, the insecure, the friendless, the outcast, the widowed, the divorced — all yearn for and need a listening ear. What a wealth of good waits to be done; what a multitude of burdens wait to be lifted if we allow God to use our ears.

I want to bring comfort to your all-pure heart wounded by sin.

ALBERT J. NIMETH, O.F.M.

□ 15 □

Notre Dame de Fourvieres—Lyons, France

The theological profile of Mary is as vast as theology itself, for she is at the very heart of the central event of theology. Her mind and her person are a prism of theology. There is reflected in her the full meaning of the Incarnation of the Son of God.

She was not only initiated, as were the Apostles and Prophets, into God's unspeakable counsel, but she wove for Him, from her own physical being, the physical fibers of His human nature. And she stood in the presence of that divine mind as it unfolded the deepest drama of human destiny.

In her role and title of God-bearer, Mother of God, is to be found the key of her riches. It is the sole source of her glory, the sole reason why "all generations shall call [her] blessed."

I offer this litany, . . .

REV. CLIFFORD STEVENS

□ 16 □

Our Lady of Victory—St. Mark, Venice

Pope Innocent XI instituted the feast of the Holy Name of Mary in 1683, to commemorate a victory over the Turks at the walls of Vienna. And an indulgence was granted to encourage devotion to the holy name of Mary.

St. Bonaventure wrote many beautiful eulogies to the name of Mary. One of these: "O salvation of all who invoke thee, I ask thee, O Mary, for the glory of thy name, to come and meet my soul when it is departing from the world, and take it in thy arms."

St. Anthony of Padua similarly wrote: "O name of Mary, joy in the heart, honey in the mouth, melody in the ear of her devout clients." Let us keep, in our hearts too, the holy name of Mary, and pray to her often, invoking her heavenly intercession.

Along with my sufferings and good works of this day, . . .

MARIE LAYNE

□ 17 □

The Virgin of Arabida—Portugal

The self-sacrifice on Mary's part is not much valued in to-day's world. In our "do-your-own-thing," and "me-first" society, self-sacrifice has been abandoned as a silly notion. Why sacrifice anything when one has made one's own self the focus of the universe?

Mary stands as a contradiction to all this. She embodies the ultimate value of Christianity—that only in losing oneself can one be reborn and live forever. As an ultimate testimony to this principle, Mary was bodily assumed into heaven. That body — with hands surely worn by a mother's work, with a heart broken too many times by pain and loss, with a head full of good ideas and common sense about human needs; that body is now to be honored as no other body ever has. Because no other body expressed so perfectly the virtues of the Gospel. Mary has been raised up, but not so high that she or the values she embodied are ever out of reach.

In reparation for the sins of the world.

JAMES MICHAEL SULLIVAN

□ 18 □

Our Lady of Fourviers

Our Blessed Mother is for all mankind, but she is extra-close to womanhood. Whether a woman belongs to the single, married, motherhood, or widowed state, she has a model who knows and understands a woman's heart.

A woman's heart is a delicate, sensitive operation. A cold, business-like world often cannot "see" the woman's point. Mary does. Do you find yourself misunderstood and suspected? Mary was. Do you find yourself burdened and weighed down with a crushing sorrow? Mary did. Have you lost an only son? Mary has.

"Go to Mary" is the secret for every woman's happiness.

Through Jesus Christ, you are the cause of our joy and the means of salvation.

PETER V. ROGERS, O.M.I.

□ 19 □

Council of Trent Confirms Feast of the Immaculate Conception

"If you love me, Simon Peter, feed my lambs, feed my sheep." These are the opening words at a feastday Mass of any Pope. Pope (St.) Pius V loved his Master. He fed His sheep; he fed His lambs in a time when the Church was overrun with many errors. He healed the wounds the Church suffered at the Reformation by enforcing the decrees of the Council of Trent.

The Church continues to bring us ever closer to a genuine, active participation in the liturgy of the Holy Sacrifice of the Mass.

I shall try to spread devotion to your Immaculate Heart . . .

MOST REV. WILLIAM T. MALLOY

Our Lady of Scheir—Bavaria

"Hail, . . .
Full of grace,"
Is the phrase
We re-echo each day
As we greet our loved Mother
In this angelic way:
Queen surpassing all women,
The great pride of our race.
Queen, full to capacity
Of God's goodness and grace.
The Almighty is with you,
Your soul free from sin—
May we keep in God's favor
And His graces win.
Among the noblest women,
None can compare to thee.
Among God's fairest angels,
There's none so fair to see.
Pray for us, holy Mary,
Both now and at death's hour;
For God
chose you Queen Mother.
With God
you have great power.

SISTER M. GEMMA BRUNKE

□ 21 □

Mary's Magnificat is the song of the truly humble person who recognizes and rejoices in God's greatness shown in His creatures. It closely parallels the song of Hannah at the birth of her son Samuel, the great prophet who was the bridge between the Judges of Israel and the Kingdom of David.

The people of Israel demanded that Samuel anoint them a king so they could be like the other nations. A thousand years later, they were still asking God for a king, a Messiah, according to the fashions of worldly success. Compared to God's magnificent plan, this desire for greatness in the eyes of the pagan nations was petty, constricting the true greatness of God's kingdom "not of this world."

"O king of the nations, the object of their yearning, the cornerstone that binds them into one! Come, save mankind whom you have fashioned out of clay."

So that many souls will find salvation in the Sacred Heart of your Son. Amen.

ANNE O'NEILL

□ 22 □

Our Lady, Queen of the Society of Jesus

It has been said that the position of women in any age is proportionate to that age's devotion to the Mother of God. Women are demanding more rights these days, but have they gained a higher position? This is a time of moral breakdown in the family, of permissive divorce and sexuality. Womankind is more of a "sex object" in our society than ever before! We need to turn to Mary, asking her to restore woman to the place of dignity that the Creator intended.

St. Ignatius of Loyola, who founded the Society of Jesus (Jesuits), had a strong devotion to our Blessed Mother. While recovering from a broken leg, he prayed before a picture of our Lady and dedicated himself to her. Thereafter, he began a new way of life, a life of prayer and poverty.

One does not usually go to the head of a political state with one's problems. It is more practical to go through other people. Likewise, Mary can be our special ambassador to God. She is the flesh-and-blood

Mother of Christ, and we can keep that in mind when we pray to her to intercede for us.

O Mary, Virgin Renowned, we pray that you intercede for us.

MARGARET HULA MALSAM

☐ 23 ☐

Veneration of the Veil and Cincture of Mary
Preserved at the Cathedral of Arras

At Nazareth, Mary and Joseph taught Jesus to walk and to talk. When He took His first step and said His first clear word, they were delighted. Many a child ends up more learned than his parents, but there is a time when they are his only teachers. So it was with Jesus.

Later, in His discourse and parables, nothing familiar to His people is missed by Him. He speaks of the wine, the oak, the fig tree, the mustard tree, the sparrow and the dove, the vipers and the wolves. He tells of the reeds and the lilies, the wheat and the cockle, the thorn and the thistles. He takes notice of the seasons, the sun and the rain, the day and the night, the stars and the storms. Nothing on which the eye might fall is left unnoticed by His word. And always with the same purpose—to enhance the greatness of the Father in the hearts and minds of His listeners. "Never has man spoken as this man."

O Mary, Mother of Jesus, help us find ways to emulate your family life.

THOMAS M. BREW, S.J.

☐ 24 ☐

Madonna of Bonaria—Sardinia

Early in life, one tradition tells us, Mary was dedicated utterly to God. She remained from childhood to serve in the Temple under the care of older women, that she might turn every moment of every day to the service and care of God's House. It was there, the story goes, that she schooled herself in the humility and obedience that were to fit her for the sublime mission in life—the divine maternity.

Our dedication to God through Christ and in the Holy Spirit took place at our baptisms. Our every Mass and Communion is an official renewal of that "belonging" to Christ and of His work for the Father. But we need something more personal than these "official" rededications. What can help all of us most to keep alert and aware of our true calling is our morning offering and repeated renewals of our good intention during the day.

O Mary, Spiritual Mother, help us to imitate your life.

REV. ROBERT L. WILKEN

□ 25 □

Mother of Good Counsel—Genazzano

I will ever remember visiting the shrine of Our Lady of Divine Love just outside of Rome. It was a Friday, November 22, 1963, the day when President Kennedy was assassinated. (May his soul rest in the peace of the Dear Lord.) Mary is called "Mother of Divine Love" because she is the Spouse of the Holy Spirit, who proceeds from the love of the Father and the Son. This feast is observed on Pentecost Sunday.

At the shrine I could sense a feeling of holiness. The favorite prayer there is: "O Virgin, Mary Immaculate, Mother of Divine Love, make us saints." May souls turn to Mary under this title and seek to grow in holiness—not extraordinary holiness, but simple, plain, good living, achieved by placing oneself in the hands of God and seeking to live as God would have all live.

O Mary, Mother of Divine Grace, help us to find fullness of grace.

MOST REV. JOHN J. CARBERRY

□ 26 □

Our Lady of Good Counsel;
The Virgin of Light—Lujan, Argentina

Mary, the gentlest of women, is also the strongest. No other woman in all human history has had any comparable influence on the minds of men. The few words that are recorded of her earthly conversation still ring in the world's ears: "How can this be since I know not man?" — virginity becomes the highest productivity. "Be it done unto me according to thy word"—the classic statement of renunciation to the will of God. "My soul doth magnify the Lord"—the world's greatest song of adoration. "Why hast thou done this to me?"—no human being, not even the purest, can altogether escape this questioning of God.

Any of Mary's words, simple as they are, can launch us into the depths of the interior life, or raise us to the heights of mysticism. They can also help us to keep our feet on the ground.

O Mary, Seat of Wisdom, make us wise to accept God's will.

REV. MSGR. J. WILLIAM MC KUNE

☐ 27 ☐

La Morencia—Montserrat, Spain

"Our Lady went into a far country. . . Our lady, for she was ours," wrote G. K. Chesterton, on the theme of the Assumption. She became Queen of Heaven, but we must not forget that she was first Queen of Earth. This feeling of closeness to the Mother of God is an instinct deep in the consciousness of Catholics—whence the multiplicity of shrines in her honor: Our lady of this and Our Lady of that, almost all of them "local" places, many of them places of pilgrimage for centuries. Chesterton sums up the devotion of Catholics toward Mary in his own unique way:

"Our Lady wears a crown in a strange country,
    The crown He gave,
But she has not forgotten to call to her old companions,
    To call and crave;
And to hear her calling a man might arise and thunder
    On the doors of the grave."

O Mary, Mother of Christ, we seek unity among all Christian peoples.

REV. CLIFFORD STEVENS

☐ 28 ☐

Visitation of Our Lady—Prague, 1263-1389

The message today seems to be "joy." In Zephaniah, we are called to "shout our joy," because we are triumphant over all our enemies—through God's power, of course. More than giving us His power, "the Lord, our God, is in our midst." We all know what it is like to clean the house for special company. How can we ever get ready for the *Lord's* coming? Rejoicing in Him is perfect preparation. It is high praise.

Some stage performers receive adulation from a clapping audience. Even greater affirmation may be given by a standing ovation, with or without cries of "Bravo!" Imagine our God exulting (one translation says "dancing") over us with joy. The paradoxes of Christianity are many, and the thought that God dances over us in joy is surely paradoxical.

Elizabeth proclaimed Mary blessed because she believed that what God said would happen. It was the word of God that Mary believed, not the words of an angel!

O Mary, Mother of God, help us to be obedient children of God.

SISTER THERESA MOLPHY, C.S.J.

□ 29 □

Our Lady of the Earthquake—Quito, Ecuador

It was through the whispering of an angel to a woman that the world's every grave was dug, every human tear salted, and the very terror of the H-bomb prepared. Michael, Gabriel, Raphael, and the rest of the angelic hosts blushed over this fact, that one of their own who had rebelled against God should have led humans into a like rebellion. But now, through Mary, God would prove Himself not only forgiving but even chivalrous toward the angelic and the human world. Instead of speaking Himself in this highest of high moments in the history of creation, God selected an angel—one of the greatest—to go down to Galilee, to a town called Nazareth, to whisper to a woman who was, like Eve, a virgin, and like Eve, destined to become the Mother of all the living but, unlike Eve, to do so without tarnishing her virginity.

O Mary, Blest among Women, we seek your help to be Christlike.

G. JOSEPH GUSTAFSON, S.S.

APRIL

□ 30 □

Our Lady of Africa—White Fathers;
Our Lady of Light—Lujan, Argentina

Because the greatness and glory of Mary have their root in Him who became her child—Jesus, the divine Son of God—it is evident that all praise and honor bestowed upon Mary finally return to God. Incomprehensible, therefore, is the objection made against Catholics that they go beyond bounds in the veneration of Mary. Do not be confused nor entertain fear in this regard. Rather, live in the childlike apprehension that you do not honor our Lady sufficiently. Trust the words of St. Bernard: "In devotion to Mary we can never do enough." Grant to the Mother of God a place of honor in your home, and (as an act of reparation for the world's neglect of her) burn a candle or light before her image on Saturdays and feast days. Never forget the words of Holy Scripture which the Church places in Mary's mouth: *They who place me in the light shall have life everlasting* (Ecclesiasticus [Sirach] 24, Douay-Rheims).

O Mary, Morning Star, we pray to see your cheering light.

KILIAN HENNRICH, O.F.M. Cap.

APRIL

M A Y

□ 1 □

St. Joseph the Worker, Spouse of the Virgin Mary

The following words of Pope Leo XIII (1878-1903) offer us much to think about concerning St. Joseph:

Joseph became the guardian, the administrator, and the legal defender of the divine house (Home of Nazareth) whose head he was. And during the whole course of his life he fulfilled those charges and those duties. He set himself to protect with mighty love and daily solicitude his spouse and the Divine Infant; regularly by his work he earned what was necessary for the one and the other for nourishment and clothing; he guarded from death the Child threatened by a monarch's jealousy, and found him a refuge; in the mysteries of the journey and in the bitterness of exile, he was ever the companion, the helper, and the upholder of the Virgin and Jesus.

Read about St. Joseph. Pray to him, and you will soon feel his intercession in your life.

O Mary, Mother of Perpetual Help, permit us not to lose faith.

MOST REV. JOHN J. CARBERRY

☐ 2 ☐

Our Lady of Oviedo—Spain

What this month of May will mean to each of us depends on our awareness of Mary in our lives and our desire to know and love her. Upon arising, our thoughts should go out to her with the prayer that we may spend the day in her honor. If possible, let us attend Holy Mass and receive our Blessed Savior in Holy Communion. During the day, even while busy, we can turn our thoughts to Mary, asking her help, sharing with her our sorrows and joys as a child does with his mother.

It is a lovely practice to place flowers before a statue of our Lady at home. Read about Mary, speak about Mary, seek to imitate Mary. Above all, however, say the Rosary daily. Upon retiring, let us again commend ourselves to her motherly care. Love of Mary will bring the greatest peace to our lives.

O Mary, Our Lady of the Miraculous Medal, help us seek grace.

MOST. REV. JOHN J. CARBERRY

☐ 3 ☐

Our Lady of Jasna Gora, Queen of the Crown of Poland;
Our Lady of Calvary—Zabrzydowska, Poland

Poland was accustomed to huge throngs at the Shrine of Our Lady near Jasna Gora. But no one had ever before witnessed what happened there in August 1956. One million pilgrims had arrived. They each had one petition. They prayed to the national Madonna for the release of the Primate, Cardinal Stefan Wyszynski, who was then being held captive in a communist prison.

They placed the cardinal's special throne, bearing his coat-of-arms, beside the altar in the shrine chapel. It was cushioned with flowers and with the national colors. In one voice, they begged Mary to fill that chair with its rightful occupant. In doing so, they were ignoring those who said they were asking for the impossible. The thunder of their prayers resounded from the shrine and its environs and was carried away on the wings of the wind.

Before the year was out, Cardinal Wyszynski was released from prison. He made a thanksgiving pilgrimage to "our Lady's mountain" at Jasna Gora. (On May 28, 1981, he was released from this life.)

O Mary, permit us to receive the promises of Christ.

ANNE TANSEY

□ 4 □

Our Lady of the Helper—near Caen, Normandy

Mary's month is a good time to reflect on what the Blessed Mother should "be" in our lives.

A *helper*. She certainly listens and lends her assistance now, as she once did at Cana in Galilee.

A *model*. She heard the word of God and kept it.

An *inspiration*. She tasted pain and felt swords of sorrow pierce her heart.

A *goal*. All generations call her blessed; and Mary's present joy more than compensates for the crosses she endured on earth.

Holy Mary, help us to follow your example of holiness.

REV. JOSEPH M. CHAMPLIN

□ 5 □

Queen of Apostles

Jesus once told His disciples that if they wanted to be great in God's Kingdom, they must learn to be the servants of all. When the Angel Gabriel told Mary she would bear God's Son, Mary answered: "I am the *servant* of the Lord. Let it be done to me as you say."

If we think of Mary as the glorious Queen of Apostles and Help of Sinners, we should remember also that she is *still* the servant of all.

Our Lord gave us another clear example of service when He washed the feet of the disciples during Passover. Afterward, He asked them if they understood what He had done for them. He told them that if such service is fitting for the Lord Himself, then so should they follow His example. And so should we.

O Mary, Queen of the Apostles, help us find people touched by the Holy Spirit.

ANN HILL

MAY

□ 6 □

Our Lady of Miracles; Our Lady of Charity

Can we ever forget the days of our childhood, when we begged favors with an almost badgering persistence? The persistence of a child who wishes to obtain a favor from mother or father is much to be admired and even imitated. A child is never satisfied with an outright "no." He learns that with each petition for a favor, the likelihood of obtaining that favor (or another one in its place) is strengthened.

Can our Mother fail to give ear to the persistence of her children when they devoutly recite her Rosary? And if the particular favor we seek is not granted, can we not be certain that Mary will reward our perseverance by asking her Divine Son to grant us another favor more in keeping with our total spiritual welfare?

If we have not in the past been faithful to the devout recitation of the Rosary, we can begin at once. If we have been faithful to this magnificent prayer, then we may rest assured that we are children of Mary.

O Mary, Mother of Good Counsel, help us find a life of salvation.

REV. LEON MC KENZIE

□ 7 □

Our Lady of Haut—Hainault, France

What is holiness? Walter J. Burghardt, S.J., expresses it in this manner: "Holiness is union with God—union with God depends upon two factors: on God and on man—on God's initiative and man's response. All holiness, all union with God, starts with God. It was God who kept sin from Mary's soul from the first moment of her existence. It was God who chose Mary to be the Virgin Mother of her Son. It was God who lifted Mary, body and soul, to unending union with Him. All union with God starts with God."

But God always asks one question: "Will you?" That is why He asked Mary, "Will you be the Mother of God?" And while the world awaited breathlessly, Mary answered: "Be it done unto me according to thy word" (Luke 1.38). May our Lady inspire us to be holy and to respond to God's invitation to holiness.

O Mary, Mother of the Savior, help us all as you promised.

MOST REV. JOHN J. CARBERRY

□ 8 □

Our Lady of Pompeii

Too often we forget that Mary offered herself to God with the same spirit that moved her divine Son. "May it be done to me according to your word."

Lord Jesus, we thank You for giving us Your Mother as You hung on the cross. We want to belong to You with all our being. Mary will teach us how. Strengthened by her example, we will confidently try to live according to Your spirit of self-sacrifice. Through Mary's intercession, may we become more like You each day.

Mary, Mother of Jesus, with your help we can be what your Son has called us to be. You have given us a mother's example of unselfish love. Set us on fire with the love of God.

O Mary, Gate of Heaven, fill our hearts with your blessed light.

LINUS MERZ, S.C.J.

□ 9 □

Mary, the Virgin Mother of Grace; Our Lady of Loreto

Mary is a queen-mother, pure and chaste, amiable and undefiled, admirable and prudent, venerable and powerful. Most of all, she is the Mother of Divine Grace. Pope Pius IX said: of her that God so enriched her from the divine treasury—far beyond all angels and the other saints—that we can hardly "conceive in thought" any greater gifts He might have given her.

Through grace we become children of God. Through grace we also can find everlasting life. Holy Mary is eager to share with us her merited, holy methods of obtaining graces promised for all souls.

O Mary, Queen of All Saints, help us to find a place among the saints.

JOHN JULIUS FISHER

MAY

□ 10 □

Our Lady of Saussai—near Paris

St. Louis de Montfort once listed the ten principal virtues of
Mary:

    her profound humility;
    her lively faith;
    her blind obedience;
    her continual mental prayer;
    her mortification in all things;
    her divine purity;
    her ardent charity;
    her heroic patience;
    her angelic sweetness;
    and her divine wisdom.

The very reading of these virtues gives rise to a certain peace of soul, a
desire for imitation, a yearning to put into practice even just one of
them. Where shall we begin? Let us ask Mary to show us the way. Very
prayerfully and sincerely, let us turn to our Lady as to our loving
Mother and select *one* of these virtues at a time for practice and devel-
opment in our souls. Our love for her, if real, should lead us to imitate
her example and follow the ideals she sets for us.

*O Mary, Cause of Our Joy, help us serve your Son with heart-filled
gladness.*

MOST REV. JOHN J. CARBERRY

□ 11 □

Vision of Our Lady to St. Philip Neri—1594

Wherever Christ is honored, Mary will be honored. Over the
years, devotion to the Mother of God has taken various forms at different times and places. One devotion that passed the test of time and is
found nearly everywhere is the Rosary.

"The Dominican Rosary of fifteen decades links our Lady to her
Son's salvific career, from the Annunciation and the joyful events of
the infancy and childhood of Jesus, through the sorrowful mysteries of
His suffering and death, to His Resurrection and Ascension, and the
sending of the Spirit to the Apostles at Pentecost, and concluding with

MAY

the Mother's reunion with her Son in the mysteries of the Assumption and Coronation.

"It is unwise to reject the Rosary without a trial simply because of the accusations that it comes from the past, that it is repetitious and ill-suited to sophisticated moderns. The scriptural riches of the Rosary are of permanent value"—*The American Bishops' Pastoral Letter on the Blessesd Virgin Mary* (November, 1973).

O Mary, Mirror of Justice, help us to live a perfect Christian life.

THOMAS M. BREW, S.J.

□ 12 □

Humility of Our Lady

In the chapel of the "old" American College in Rome (as distinguished from the "new" college built after the war), there hung over the altar a picture known as "Our Lady of Humility." Artistically it was perhaps not outstanding; but the students of the college came to love it and prayed earnestly to Our Lady of Humility.

True humility is stark honesty. It means to give God His place in our lives, and to acknowledge that whatever gift we may have comes from Him. Mary had true humility. She was aware that she had many graces; and she even said, "All generations will call me blessed." More important, however, was the fact that she believed that of herself she was nothing and that God was all.

The proud of heart do not know lasting peace of soul. They lose themselves in the darkness of self-seeking. In the humble soul, however, true peace reigns.

O Mary Immaculate, we always need your aid and interceding help.

MOST REV. JOHN J. CARBERRY

□ 13 □

Our Lady of Fatima

On May 13, 1917, during the First World War, the Blessed Virgin appeared to three children in Fatima, Portugal. She told the children to give the world a message that would bring the war to an end. The message asked for the recitation of the daily Rosary, Mass and

Communion on five First Saturdays, and daily penance. Portugal and Ireland heeded the message and lived it. They were not involved in the Second World War.

The Blessed Virgin told the children, "If my message is not heeded, there will be another most terrible war, whole nations will be annihilated, communism will spread; but in the end my Immaculate Heart will triumph, Russia will be converted, and there will be an era of peace."

Is the triumph near? Are there a sufficient number saying the daily Rosary? More than six decades have come and gone. Something to think about.

O Mary, Queen of Peace, let us be a part of your world-peace movement.

TOM MARTIN, S.J.

□ 14 □

Our Lady, Patroness of Bavaria—Munich

Some of my earliest recollections of Mother's Day include a statue of the Madonna enshrined on a bedside table. The doll-sized statue was framed with freshly cut flowers—lilacs, tulips, and lilies of the valley. Mary's crown was one of violets, woven in prayer by my invalid mother.

Marian hymns we learned from saintly and dedicated "Sister Marys," who also helped us craft the familiar spiritual bouquets for our mothers for Mother's Day. In our parish, Mother's Day was also the traditional First Communion day for the second graders. My own children followed that same tradition.

Pope John Paul II once said: "Motherhood is the vocation of the woman—eternal and contemporary—as it was for Mary, the mother of all men." It is no wonder that mothers rate a special holiday.

O Mary, Mother Most Pure, help us to put motherhood on a sacred basis.

PATRICK R. MORAN

□ 15 □

Mother of Divine Grace—England and Wales;
Our Lady, Patroness of France

Devotion to the Sacred Heart of Jesus really honors our Lord's love for us; this devotion is bound closely to the Passion. Likewise, devotion to the Immaculate Heart of Mary is a way of acknowledging her love for us; and it too is related to the Passion. Mary's role is now one of intercession. That is what any good mother does—plead with the "powers that be" for her children. What more powerful voice can we find before the throne of Almighty God, whose Son on earth was subject to her as a child? When Mary heard from the cross, "Woman, there is your son," she knew that she was appointed to be mother of all the followers of Christ.

What we ask through her, and what she petitions God on our behalf, is grace. That is why "grace" is the recurring note struck during the prayers of this day's Mass.

O Mary, Blessed by the Holy Spirit, help us to find the Holy Spirit.

REV. MSGR. JAMES I. TUCEK

□ 16 □

Vision of Our Lady by St. Catherine of Alexandria

Jacinta, one of the children of Fatima, although only nine years old at the time, died alone in a hospital far from her home. The Virgin had told her it would be so, but said she would come for her on a stated day and at a certain hour. Before leaving Fatima to enter the hospital, Jacinta talked with her cousin Lucy and expressed a great fear of dying alone. In reassurance, her cousin said to her: "What do you care if you die alone, Jacinta, if our Lady is coming to take you?"

We will most assuredly not die alone, no matter where we are, or in what circumstances, if we have formed the habit of repeating, morning and evening, the aspiration, "Jesus, Mary, and Joseph, may I die in your blessed arms." In their holy company, what would we have to fear?

O Mary, Mystical Rose, we pray that more saints arise among us.

ROBERT J. LEUVER, C.M.F.

□ 17 □

Madonna of Tears—Duchy of Spoleto, Italy

Mary shared the range of feelings voiced by Jesus as He hung on the cross: forgiveness for those who sin without knowing what they do; pardon for one who asked for it; physical thirst, as well as spiritual thirst for the salvation of all; desolation over the monstrous evil of sin, which shuts God out of human life and leaves it empty and wasted; final realization that the agony was over; and total commendation of self to God the Father, in the pattern of a life surrendered entirely to Him.

Mary experienced not only the sentiments of Jesus but also the grief that only a mother can know at the death of a son. It was the price she paid for her maternity. The sword cut deeply, as Simeon had said it would, matching the thrust of the other sword into the heart of Jesus.

O Mary, Comforter of the Afflicted, be our comfort.

FELICIAN A. FOY, O.F.M.

□ 18 □

Notre Dame de Bonport—France

It is most fitting that Mary, who was to be the Mother of Christ, should be exempt from the worst effects that Adam's sin had bequeathed to the human race. The poet William Wordsworth called her "Our tainted nature's solitary boast," meaning that she alone was spared from the stain of Adam's sin.

Catholics believe that the fruits of the Redemption were applied to Mary when she was created—hence we honor her under the title of her Immaculate Conception. It would be incongruous for the Son of God to be born of a woman who was tainted by sin. Just as our Redeemer is adored by Christians, is it not fitting that they should His Mother? We honor her today because she is indeed "our tainted nature's solitary boast."

O Mary, Mother Most Chaste, help us to live chaste lives.

JOHN M. MARTIN, M.M.

□ 19 □

Notre Dame de Flines—France

In the carrying out of His plan for the human race, God has peopled history with rare personalities, magnificent partial mirrors of His own mind and person. Moses, David, the prophets, Paul—all embody something of the vastness and magnitude of God the Creator.

It is no small wonder that artists, sculptors, and poets have tried to capture or express something of the rich significance of Mary; for, in a sense, she is a synthesis of the Old and New Covenants. In her, first and uniquely, are God's ancient promises fulfilled and new promises made. She captures in her person, and in her God-bearing, the full significance of priest, prophet, and apostle and is a shining monument of the action of God in human history.

O Mary, Refuge of Sinners, let us help you in your work.

REV. CLIFFORD STEVENS

□ 20 □

Queen of the Clergy

Our Blessed Lady was neither a priest nor bishop. Queen of the Clergy though she is, she did not forgive sins or celebrate Mass. She was, rather, the Church's ideal parishioner!

Hurrying to help her cousin Elizabeth, she was compassionate. Concerned over the plight of the newlyweds at Cana, she was considerate. In the Acts of the Apostles, we find one line describing her in that first apostolic parish: "The Apostles with one mind continued steadfastly in prayer with the women, and Mary the Mother of Jesus." This harmony of public prayer and private kindness, we must seek.

Heavenly Mother, teach us to want neither praise nor attention but only to be instruments of the grace of salvation.

MOST REV. PAUL J. HALLINAN

□ 21 □

Our Lady of Wladimir—Russia;
Our Lady of the Cenacle

The first Saturday of each month has been set aside to honor the Immaculate Heart of Mary. This was one result of the Fatima appearances of our Lady, when she spoke of the Communion of reparation, which she wanted made on the first Saturday of each month.

Reparation for sin is something we seldom think about. We express sorrow for our own misdeeds in the Sacrament of Reconciliation, perform some small penance, then forget about them. We forget that it is one thing to have sin forgiven, and quite another to eradicate temporal punishment due for our sins.

We can make reparation for sin through many means: Mass, sacraments, prayer, acts of love and self-denial. We are not limited to reparation for our own sins either. God will accept our acts of reparation for the sins of others. Mary, knowing this need for reparation, asks for it from us. Can we refuse her?

Immaculate Heart of Mary, be my refuge when I repent, my strength in temptation, and my guide toward heaven.

WILLIAM J. NEIDHART, C.S.C.

□ 22 □

Our Lady of the Virgin's Mount—Naples

May is rightly regarded as one of the more beautiful months of the year. It's as though it were designed solely for artists, poets, lyricists, and photographers, as all the springtime delights of this month have been the theme of numerous paintings, sonnets, songs, and photographs.

For some reason, May has also been the first word in many an infant's vocabulary. Perhaps in sounding the word there is a similarity to the sounds of *ma, ma-ma, mae,* or *Mary.* Then too, the sounds that make up the name of Mary have a natural tonal beauty. The innocence and spiritual beauty of an infant daughter or son may well appreciate that quality. In any case, May is truly Mary's month, as we "crown her with blossoms"—Queen of the Angels, Queen of the May.

O loving Mother Mary, be my model and inspiration!

PATRICK R. MORAN

MAY

☐ 23 ☐

Our Lady of the Miracles—St. Omer, Belgium

"True devotion to our Lady makes us her instruments and co-workers in the invisible birth of Jesus Christ and the unfolding of His life in souls," according to Cardinal Leo Josef Suenens, of Belgium (writing in *The Marian Era.*) The Cardinal said that Mary wants more than mere devotion. She wants our *collaboration* in apostolic labors. Church tradition has long held that Mary worked with the Apostles in the building of the Church that Jesus had founded. She was not a mere onlooker. Jesus had made her the mother of humankind, thus giving her a worldwide mission for all times.

Like all mothers, she wants to help us. But she expects help from her children. We can assist in carrying out her own inscrutable plans—such as by being attentive to her messages. Those who are attentive are often amazed at the tasks she wants performed, and yet at how even difficult missions can be carried out if her guidance is accepted.

O Mary, conceived without sin, pray for us who have recourse to thee!

ANNE TANSEY

☐ 24 ☐

Our Lady, Help of Christians;
Our Lady of the Highway

The Catholic Church has been at war with Satan and his evil forces since its institution. All Christians should seek Mary's help in fighting against those forces that pervert truth, corrupt morals, and persecute the innocent.

Mary has been the "Help of Christians" many times in the past when evil forces were trying to destroy the Church. Through her spiritual intercession, the cunning, cruel and inhuman forces were finally put down.

Mary is both the Mother of Eternal Truth, and Conqueror of the world of sin. Her Son can help us receive justice, love, and peace. She has given many signs that her power and help are forthcoming to all her spiritual children.

O, Mary, Help of Christians, enlighten the blindness of our self-centered world.

□ 25 □

Our Lady of New Jerusalem

There is a striking line in the beautiful poem "Limbo" by Sister Mary Ada. When word comes that the Risen Christ will visit Limbo, all the saints are excited. Moses asks David to prepare a welcome song and the "three youths" to sing the *Benedicite*. Suddenly Christ appears, and none can speak, "confused with joy." A silent man, alone of all, found tongue. Old Joseph said: "How is your Mother, Son?"

Joseph loved Mary, and she loved him. It would not have been a holy family if they hadn't. It was the kind of love that could contain tender care (as at Bethlehem), full trust (as in Nazareth), and constant concern (as in Egypt). They loved each other, and this made their sacrifice to God's will, their chastity, more marvelous and more splendid.

No home can be holy without love. But no love can be holy unless it makes room for God first.

Mother of Christ, Mother of Christ: What shall I ask of thee?

MOST REV. PAUL J. HALLINAN

□ 26 □

Notre Dame de Vaucelles—France;
Madonna of Caravaggio

We are all led to imitate what we admire but, after all, the greatest transforming power is love. One spark of love will help us to understand our Blessed Mother, and to form ourselves in her image, more than a whole library of theological books. Our minds need to be enlightened by the truths of faith; but in an unbelieving age, our hearts also need to be touched. Mary, our mother, will do that.

It is remarkable that the saints were not only devoted to Christ's Mother, but grew in devotion to her as their holiness increased. Their love for Mary kept pace, as it were, with their love for her Son. The more they came to know God and the better they loved Him, the greater became their appreciation of His Mother, and their love for her also grew.

Can we who are not saints afford to neglect Mary's powerful intercession, on which they relied so much?

O Mary, Mother Amiable, help us to increase our love for all.

ALBERT A. MURRAY, C.S.P.

☐ 27 ☐

Notre Dame de Napoes—France

"A joy shared is a joy doubled; a sorrow shared is a sorrow halved." Most of us have known this experience; we received a promotion at work—a new baby was expected—good news came through the mail. ... Somehow the joy was not complete until we had shared it with a friend. In times of sadness, the sympathetic ear of a friend brought consolation: grief shared became bearable.

Mary was delightfully human: no sooner had she received the "good news" from the angel than she was off to share it with Elizabeth. Even our Lord sought human companionship in the garden of betrayal.

Mary, help me remember that "no man is an island." Others need me, I need others. Take me out of the shadows of loneliness and into the light of love.

O Mary, Health of the Sick, we pray you will always tend our needs.

DIANNE RUSSELL

☐ 28 ☐

Feast of the Relics of Our Lady—Venice, Italy

Seven sorrows there were, which stabbed the heart of Mary! Other painful and anxious moments could no doubt be listed, but these seven could be experienced by no other human—for Mary was the Mother of God, and her sorrow was inflicted on her by what the sins of man would do to her Son. ...

MAY

Simeon's prophecy
  Flight into Egypt
    Loss in the Temple
      Meeting Jesus on the Way to Calvary
        Crucifixion of Jesus
          Removal from the Cross
          Burial of Jesus

There was no selfish sorrow in Mary. She could think only of her Son. it was the events in Christ's life, her Son, her flesh and blood, that caused her pain. . .and this only because she willed to be a part of her Son's Redemptive life.

Let us waste no time on useless self-pity!

O Mary, Mediatrix and Co-redemptrix, pray for us.

MOST REV. ALBERT R. ZUROWESTE

□ 29 □

Our Lady of the Cross—Carcassone, France

The thought of the sacred body of our Lord descending from the cross into our Lady's arms turns our minds to our past lives, where, as in His many wounds, we may read the story of our failures and infidelities to grace. There is the spittle of the scorn with which gracious calls to virtue have been rejected. There are the bruises left by our want of kindness to others. There are the open wounds of willful offenses against God. The burden is too great for us to bear; so let us carry it to our Lady, in St. Peter's spirit of humble shame.

Fresh life, born of the pardon of God and the peace of Christ, will rise within us, dispelling all discouragement. A resting place for our past life, with all the thoughts it suggests, and all the regrets it brings, is a need for us all. The Heart of Mary can ease its sting and help us to bear its burden.

When the evening of Good Friday came, our Lord's body was taken down from the cross and laid in the arms of His Mother. Let the evening of each day in this vale of tears be spent in the company of our Lady, the Mother of Sorrows. For she is also the Mother of holy hope, and she will pour out for us on each day's work the oil of gladness to heal all blemishes and to bless and encourage yet further work for God on the morrow. Thus we may confidently expect that, having sown in tears, we may reap in joy, and that by the healing of the Precious Blood sinners may be turned into saints.

The sacred Passion, as the instrument of man's Redemption, was always the theme of Mary's thoughts and prayers. Her Son gave her a new office, a new name, and a new dignity when He said to her from the cross: "Woman, behold thy son." She is now our mother; she looks upon us all as her children, for whom she labors that Christ may be formed in us.

O Mary, our hope, have pity on us!

MOST REV. RICHARD J. CUSHING

□ 30 □

Mother of Fair Love

On this beautiful feast of our Lady, we naturally turn to her for comfort and consolation. Surely she will remember her poor exiled children here on earth.

Mother, you must surely know how we still suffer, your human heart must still have some thought and pity for your poor children in this vale of tears. Pity those who weep in sorrow. Pity those who have loved and lost. Pity those who are in the dark, blindly groping for the truth. Pity those whose hearts are dead, poisoned by the selfish world. Pity those who are weak and wayward. Pity those who are obdurate. Pity us all, for you are the Mother of Jesus, and we are the poor lost children, for whose Redemption He gave His blood and His Mother.

Mother, you do love us. You are our Queen, but we have a right to call you mother. Have pity on us; give us this day the blessing of your Son; and bring us safely home to Him.

Hail, Holy Queen, our life, our sweetness, our hope!

ALBERT A. MURRAY, C.S.P.

□ 31 □

The Visitation

Today we end the month of May by honoring Mary as we commemorate her visit to Elizabeth, which provides us with many lessons. Mary goes out of her way to help another. Do *we*? Mary spreads the good news of salvation. Do *we*? John stirs in the womb of Elizabeth because he senses the presence of God in Mary. Do other people have the same reaction to us?

Mary stands as a woman of faith, undaunted by consistently negative circumstances in her life. She rose above every limitation and became a truly liberated woman—not through egocentricity, self-assertion, or a petty clinging to personal rights, but by giving herself over totally to God.

The Gospels give us only one instance of Mary's giving directives; but that one is sufficient: "Do whatever he tells you" (John 2.5). That one injunction is a task of a lifetime. She excelled in taking her own advice. That is why every generation of Christians has fulfilled her prophecy, by calling her "blessed."

Our Lady of the Rosary, pray for us.

REV. MR. PETER M. STRAVINSKAS

MAY

JUNE

□ 1 □

Our Lady, Health of the Sick — Kevelaer, Germany

Mary was Christ's parting gift, given to us moments before He died. She is one more example of the excesses of God's generosity to man. Redemption could have been accomplished without her. But God chose her to be intimately bound up in the divine plan. The Word was made flesh through her flesh, and both are at this moment in heaven, the One ascended, the other assumed.

Think of man's notions of God under the Old Law and then compare this with man's relation to God in the New Law. The words of the scriptures show the difference plainly. Formerly God was a tremendous majesty, an avenging God, an exacting and unbending judge. If we see God now in gentler terms, it is in great part due to the "woman's touch." If God appears now as a Father, it is because we have Mary as Mother.

Holy Mary, Mother of God, pray for us, now and at the hour of our death.

REV. MSGR. JAMES. I. TUCEK

□ 2 □

Our Lady of Edessa — Asia Minor

Mary's Canticle is a song of affirmation. Mary wholly accepts herself for who and what she is. Honestly and happily she admits to being humble. Boldly but truthfuly she announces an "unthinkable" prophecy: "All ages shall call me blessed!" As the crowds said of Christ: "No man has ever spoken as this man!" so too, can it be said: "No woman has ever spoken as this woman!"

Being humble, Mary acknowledges, in the same breath, the source of her uniqueness and holiness: "God has done great things for me." She realizes God "raises the lowly to high places." Her lowliness has won her God's favor. To a far lesser degree can the affirming words of Mary be reechoed by us. If we become holy, we will be held in blessed memory. If we accept who and what we are, God will affirm us by His mighty graces. We will sing a Canticle proclaiming God's greatness.

O, Mary, show thyself a Mother to me.

BRUCE RISKI, O.F.M. Cap.

□ 3 □

Our Lady of Sosopoli — in Pisidia

Few ideals have caused so many wars as peace. The trouble is that it is only peace on our terms that we want. Our Lady of Fatima warned us to pray and do penance to escape the scourge of war. Have you ever watched a group of children daringly getting deeper into trouble and thought, "They're really asking for it"?

But on the more personal level, where most of us live, are we peacemakers? "A gentle answer turneth away wrath." Gentle answers like — "I'm sorry. I did not mean to hurt you." — "Why are you angry?" — "Can I help?" — "Yes, you probably are right." — "I can't agree with you, but you don't have to agree with me either, you know." — "I didn't know that habit of mine bugged you." — "O.K. Let's try it your way." Use gentle words. "Thank you." — "Congratulations." — "I love you."

Resolve that nothing will interfere with our daily recitation of the Rosary.

TERRY MARTIN

JUNE

□ 4 □

Madonna of the Hill — Fribourg, Switzerland

Many travelers who took a winding path in the Swiss Alps were never heard of again. Occasionally a body would be found in some rock-strewn canyon. The Alpine villagers lost count of the hunters, shepherds, farmers, travelers, and pilgrims who perished before reaching the top of the mountain.

Searching for a solution, the villagers finally decided to dedicate the path to Mary. They built a chapel in her honor on the most treacherous strip. Men risked their lives and limbs carrying tools and lumber to the slope while facing gorges on either side and massive rock formations overhead.

At its completion a priest led a procession carrying a picture of the Virgin to enshrine in the newly blessed chapel dedicated to Our Lady of the Wanderers. Thereafter, all who came that way had a place in which to rest and pray for their protection. Some saw in it a symbol of the spiritual life.

O Mary, I am all thine.

ANNE TANSEY

□ 5 □

St. Mary in Cosmedin — Rome

May, Mary's month, is followed by the month dedicated to the Sacred Heart of Jesus. Thus it should be, for Mary leads us to Jesus. That is her role. If in the month of May we gave special thoughts to our Blessed Mother, then it will not be difficult to turn our thoughts to the Sacred Heart in June. For devotion to Mary, if it is true, if it does her honor, if it is pleasing to her, will not stop with her.

In the Gospel, Mary's role is clearly indicated. She is mentioned only a few times, and then only in her relation to her Son. At Bethlehem she "brought forth her first born" and presented Him to shepherd and Magi. At Cana she introduced Him to the public. On Calvary she suffered with Him and she offered with Him.

At Mary's side we shall learn what it means to love the Sacred Heart.

O Mary, keep me, guard me as thy property and thy possession.

MOST REV. HENRY A. PINGER, O.F.M. (China)

JUNE

☐ 6 ☐

Founding of the Nuns of the Visitation of Our Lady — 1610

The feast of the Visitation revolves about two mothers-to-be, Mary and her cousin Elizabeth. They had so much in common. A stream of understanding flowed between them, independent of words. Each knew the other's thoughts and feelings. To the natural closeness that existed between the two, a new bond was added.

As Mary understood Elizabeth, Mary understands us, because every joy and sorrow we know can find its twin in her life. She knew the small trials — money problems (a carpenter's job was not always a steady one) — trouble with relatives (they rejected her Son and His teachings). There were the major sorrows, too — the loss of her husband; the suffering and death of her Son.

Mary is qualified to be our understanding confidante in every hardship. She knows how we feel. She lived it all herself.

My Mother, I leave myself in your hands; do with me what you wish.

REV. LEO J. TRESE

☐ 7 ☐

Our Lady of the Valley

Drive north from Jerusalem for about twenty-five minutes, and you will come to the ruins of a *khan*, an inn and resting place for caravans which, in ancient times, needed one day's journey to reach here from the Holy City. An excellent spring still refreshes the traveler. It is enshrined by one of the most honored mosques in Islam, a house of Muslim prayer that actually commemorates the family of Christ.

This is the place where Joseph and Mary, returning from the Passover in Jerusalem, would have first noticed that the twelve-year-old Jesus was not among relatives in the caravan. From here, they departed in the night to retrace their steps — and found Him teaching among the doctors of the Temple.

How many of us can go a day's journey without losing the sense of the presence of Christ?

Mother, may all who look at me, see you.

REV. MSGR. JOHN G. NOLAN

□ 8 □

Our Lady of Wisdom

Mary is called "Seat of Wisdom" because she is the Mother of the Incarnate Divine Wisdom, our Lord and Savior, Jesus Christ.

The Holy Spirit infused into her soul the fullness of His gifts, the first was wisdom. Mary possessed wisdom in the highest degree; she is, one can say, the storehouse of whatever wisdom we need in the attainment of our purpose in life.

In times of doubt, worry, or indecision, whisper to our Lady, "Mary, Seat of Wisdom, pray for us." She will answer; have no doubts. She will obtain the grace that we may see what God would have us do. She will refine our sense of values, she will show us how passing are the pleasures of the world and the emptiness of its honors; she will help us appreciate the purpose of life — to know, love, and serve God. This is wisdom!

My Queen and my Mother, teach me how to pray to you.

MOST. REV. JOHN J. CARBERRY

□ 9 □

Mother of Divine Grace — United States of America

Loyal and loving devotion to our Lady has been a part of American life from the beginning. In 1847 papal approval was given to the request that Mary, under the title of the Immaculate Conception, be named patroness of the United States. Numerous cathedrals, churches, and institutions of higher learning bear Mary's titles.

This precious heritage is ours to pass on to succeeding generations, but are we doing so?

A decline in devotion to Mary was noted by the American bishops in their 1973 pastoral letter: "No survey is needed to show that all over the country many forms of Marian devotion have fallen into disuse. . . .We view with great sympathy the distress our people feel over this . . . and we share their concern that the young be taught a deep and true love for the Mother of God." Disappointing as this is, it should become a challenge to Mary's people to pray more and work harder.

Beloved Mother Mary, show me the way to consecrate my total being to your beloved Son, Jesus.

THOMAS M. BREW, S.J.

JUNE

□ 10 □

Madonna of Cranganor — East Indies

Cardinal Newman had a beautiful devotion to the Blessed Mother, as did every saintly person who has preceded us in life. Surely, this should be a lesson for us all. Archbishop Sheen once wrote: "It is a constant tradition of the Catholic Church that anyone who is truly devoted to the Blessed Mother is never lost."

Cardinal Newman wrote: "O Mary, abide with us, who are your children; guide us along the path which leads to God. Be to us always a Mother." The Cardinal especially asked our Heavenly Mother to "make our priests blameless and beyond reproach." Let this be our prayer too, for we need good priests: a church is just a hall without priests.

Love of Mary leads to love of Christ.

REV. RAWLEY MYERS

□ 11 □

Immaculate Heart of Mary

The heart has always been used symbolically as the center of life and love. In the Immaculate Hearts of Jesus and Mary we have the perfect example of God's love for man and man's love for his fellowmen.

Nobody ever loved her fellowmen as our Blessed Mother, to whom our Lord committed the entire human race, when dying on the cross.

Mary has an obligation toward us as a mother has toward her children. We have a right with Mary just as the children have a right to their parents. We can turn confidently to her in prayer, knowing that she will fulfill her duty as our Mother.

Sweet heart of Jesus, be my love; Sweet heart of Mary, be my salvation.

REV. MSGR. JOSEPH B. LUX

□ 12 □

Vision of Our Lady to St. Herman

Mary is surely the closest person to Jesus. Like the saints of the Old Testament she too was looking forward to and praying for the fulfillment of God's promise to His people.

When the Angel Gabriel greeted her with the extraordinary words, "Hail, full of grace," and told her that she was to be the mother of the coming "son of David" she understood and accepted the full implication of this privilege by uttering the beautiful words: "Behold the handmaid of the Lord, be it done to me according to your word."

Such understanding and acceptance shows that Mary was accustomed to meditate on the promises and steps of salvation history as they had been revealed to Israel and written in scripture. Mary's response to the angel's message shows that God also had been preparing her in a special way for the great event.

Our Lady of the Rosary of Fatima, pray for us!

MARTIN SCHOENBERG, O.S.C.

□ 13 □

Madonna of Sichem — near Louvain

"We are tossed on the tempest of the sea," St. Bernard says. "The sea which threatens to swallow us up. Amid the winds of temptation and the waves of tribulation, we dread judgment and fear because of our sins. And sometimes we are plunged into the gulf of sadness as the anguish of doubt assails us."

What must we do? Bernard goes on: "Then, let the name of Mary, Star of the Sea, be on your lips and in your heart. She will sustain you and give you hope. By her help you will reach the port of safety."

As another writer wrote: "She is the Mother of all living, hope for the weak, comforter of the afflicted."

Let our approach to Mary be childlike, and devotion will follow.

REV. RAWLEY MYERS

☐ 14 ☐

Our Lady of Treille — Lille

We must never think that the Blessed Virgin had an easy life. If anything is clear in the Gospels, it is that the Blessed Virgin's condition, as far as her experience went, was very similar to ours. She had to work out her salvation.

She enjoyed no privileges that would make things easier. The apparently "harsh" words which our Lord addressed to her were obviously intended to show that her role as His Mother did not exempt her from playing the normal part of a pilgrim on earth hoping for the happiness of heaven.

"Did you not know that I must be about my Father's business?" is a clear statement, setting the record straight. This must have been a little hard for Mary to understand. It must have been hard for her to "find her place" in our Lord's life. But she met the problem with courage, keeping "all these things in her heart."

O Virgin Mary, Mother of Divine Love, make us saints.

REV. MSGR. J. WILLIAM MC KUNE

☐ 15 ☐

Dedication of First Church to Mary — Syrians

The Holy Family at Nazareth is the model for all families. In that humble home peace, holiness, and love reigned supreme.

The home is the bedrock of society, the foundation upon which civilization reposes. Blast at the home with the atomic bomb of divorce and you destroy the foundation of Christian life and civilization.

The number of unhappy American homes has increased enormously in recent years. Lots of reasons are cited for this. But there is only one real reason: namely, the fact that marriage, the family, the home are less and less centered in God, related to God, permeated by God. A wheel falls to pieces without a hub, and a home falls to pieces without God. A body dies without a heart, and a home dies unless God is its heart.

True happiness is to be found in holiness.

REV. JOHN A. O'BRIEN

□ 16 □

Our Lady of Aix-la-Chapelle — Germany

Have you ever felt all alone? No one interested in you. . .no one to care whether you live or die! You just feel abandoned! You pray, but nothing happens as even your prayers are drier than dry and seem thoroughly unproductive. Well, think again!

Our Lord never forsakes us! Nor does our Blessed Mother in whose *Memorare* we recognize that she never leaves us unprotected, unaided. . .nor does our Guardian Angel. . .nor do our patron saints. . .nor do the other angels and saints. . .nor do those once Poor Souls whom our prayers helped to reach heaven. . .nor do those still Poor Souls who are advancing closer to heaven through our prayers. . .nor do our associates in the world united with us in the Communion of Saints! So, who's all alone?

God is certainly most good to us. Regrettably, there is not enough time in a whole lifetime to adequately thank and praise Him.

May the invocation "Mary, my Queen and my Mother" be our frequent prayer.

REV. MSGR. RALPH G. KUTZ

□ 17 □

Madonna of the Forest — near Boulogne-sur-Mer

We ask the prayers of Mary because God in His word has told us to do so.

Could anything be clearer? Why was it that God Incarnate waited so long to show the signs of His divinity?

He waited until he was a mature man. Then His Mother asked Him to perform a miracle. She told Him there was no more wine at the marriage feast and in the telling there was the asking. But our Lord was not ready to show Himself. His time had not yet come, He told His Mother.

But she, like a mother who knew her Son, did not accept His protest. Even though He did not wish it, she wanted Him to do this favor for her.

So He did it. His first miracle on earth was performed against His own wish because His Mother wanted it.

It is not strange that we ask for help, it is only strange that all men do not do so.

He said to His Mother, "Woman, behold thy Son."

DALE FRANCIS

□ 18 □

Vision of Our Lady by St. Agnes of Mount Politian

"One thing in particular, and that indeed one of great importance, we specially desire that all should pray for, under the auspices of our heavenly Queen. That is, that she, who is loved and venerated with such ardent piety, would not suffer them to wander and be unhappily led further away from the unity of the Church, and therefore from her Son whose vicar on earth we are.

"May they return to the common Father, whose judgment all the fathers in the synod of Ephesus most dutifully received; may they all return to us, who have indeed a fatherly affection for them all, and who gladly make our own those most loving words which Cyril used, when he earnestly exhorted Nestorius that 'the peace of the churches may be preserved, and that the bond of love and of concord among the priests of God may remain indissoluble' " — Pius XI, Encyclical, *Lux Veritatis.*

May she see in all of us her own features of holiness.

G. JOSEPH GUSTAFSON, S.S.

□ 19 □

Veneration of Our Lady's Comb at Church
of St. John the Evangelist — Treves, Germany

It may be a bit difficult to conceive the idea of the Mother of God doing such things as cooking meals, washing dishes, and the like, At Nazareth Mary found her days taken up with most of the works of the "vigorous wife," described in the thirty-first chapter of the Book of Proverbs. All that could be done in the home she did. And she never lost contact with God, God in her soul, God playing on the floor.

The tasks of life await us daily, hourly, and we would be wise to take them as they are. They might have been otherwise and they might have been more to our liking.

JUNE

One hundred years from now it will make no difference whether we stood high or low, whether we did big things or the small things that are the lot of most people's lives. What will matter then is the way they were done. Not the "what" of our lives but the "how" is what will count.

Our Lady of Humility, teach us to be humble of heart!

THOMAS M. BREW, S.J.

□ 20 □

Madonna of Consolation — Turin

Our Lady, Co-Redemptress—"The Virgin of Sorrows," wrote Pope Pius XI in 1923, "participated with Christ in the work of the redemption."

Men are mistaken who see our Lady merely as the Child-bearer and the caretaker. Mary's life follows a pattern of fiery charity, of spiritual grandeur, with distinctly missionary objective, namely to cooperate in the Incarnation for the saving of mankind and in the Redemption to satisfy for mankind.

Mary possesses spiritual loveliness: intelligence that is pure and keen, a will that has never failed, a soul that is exquisitely sensitive, altogether the quality of admirableness — *mater admirabilis*. Mary is inextricably bound up with Christ the Priest. His great role of Redeemer is a sacerdotal role; hers is to be the Mother, but Co-Redemptress as well. Mary was not a mere weeper on Calvary. At every Mass there is the same union between her and Jesus for the world's redemption.

Like Mary may we know the Holy Spirit and be attentive to His inspirations.

JOHN J. CONSIDINE, M.M.

□ 21 □

Our Lady of Attrib — Egypt

Pope Paul VI, at the closing of the third session of the Second Vatican Council (Nov. 21, 1964), proclaimed: "For the glory of the Virgin Mary and for our own consolation, we proclaim the Most Blessed Virgin Mary Mother of the Church, that is to say of all the People of

God, of the faithful as well as of the pastors, who call her the most loving Mother.

"We desire that the Mother of God should be still more honored and invoked by the entire Christian people by this most sweet title.

"O Mary, to your Immaculate Heart we recommend the entire human race. Lead it to the knowledge of the sole and true Savior, Jesus Christ. Protect it from the scourges provoked by sin, give to the entire world peace, in truth, in justice, in liberty and in love."

Mary Queen of Peace, fill my soul with the peace of Christ!

PASCHAL BOLAND, O.S.B.

□ 22 □

Our Lady of Narmi — Italy

Devotion to Mary stretches back to the early years of the Church's life. The veneration and affection of the saints for Mary was an expression of the love for her Son which filled their hearts. And so it is always in the Church: devotion to the Blessed Virgin Mary brings us closer to Christ.

Our Lady is the exemplar of the Christian life. Her own life was far from easy. With faith and perseverance she carried through. Her whole existence was a response to God's call. She mirrors the response the whole Church is called upon to make. It would be a mistake, though, if we did not realize that Mary had to walk a similar path to ourselves. She was uniquely privileged, as the Mother of God made man, but that did not exempt her from effort, from the search for God's will. She understands our efforts; she prays with us and on our behalf. The Hail Mary should be on our lips and in our hearts today.

Immaculate Heart of Mary, pray for us.

REV. MSGR. PETER COUGHLAN

□ 23 □

Our Lady of Wladimir — Moscow, Russia

The commemoration of the feast of the Immaculate Heart of Mary, now an optional memorial, was originally ordered by Pope Pius XII (May 4, 1944), for observance throughout the Church in order to obtain Mary's intercession for "peace among nations, freedom for the Church, the conversion of sinners, the love of purity and the practice of virtue." Two years earlier the Holy Father consecrated all peoples to Mary under the title of her Immaculate Heart.

The pope's intentions were related to those that had been suggested by Mary during two appearances to two French children at LaSalette in 1846; to St. Bernadette at Lourdes in 1858, and to three Portuguese children at Fatima in 1917. The urgency of the intentions, which have been recommended in numerous pastoral statements, is undeniable.

We all share in the Church ministry of prayer, not only with and for those who profess our faith but also for the good of all peoples.

O Mary, Madonna of America, help us.

FELICIAN A. FOY, O.F.M.

□ 24 □

Our Lady of the Clos-Evrard — Treves, Germany

From the moment she became the Mother of God, Mary became the mediatrix between man and God. (A mediatrix is one who unites, who brings together two separated persons.) Jesus, the Son of God, is placed as mediator between God and Man. St. John says He is our advocate with the Father. He constantly intercedes for sinners. Christ, in becoming man, and making Himself our mediator, has not ceased to be God. Our sins have offended each of the three Divine Persons. Therefore, we have offended our mediator. We, therefore, need someone who has never offended Him by any sin, to mediate between Him and us.

St. Bernard tells us: "It is Mary. She is the person most capable of inclining God, her Son, to be merciful and clement toward us. God has even appointed her to fulfill this charitable role of mediatrix between Himself and men. He has given her the power to speak of holy violence whereby she can withhold His hands when He is ready to punish His children. Jesus is calmed more quickly by Mary than by any other intercessor, including an angel."

Mystical Rose, pray for us!

MARIE LAYNE

JUNE

□ 25 □

Mary Declared to Be the Mother of God
by Council of Ephesus

Mary, as the Mother of God, was proclaimed on June 22, 431. The Council of the Catholic Church solemnly defined that the title Mother of God must be given our Lady. This title was instituted to further the devotion held for Jesus, our Savior, to declare His divinity.

Mary, throughout the years, has come to be a dedicated spiritual Mother for all Christians. She has taken her rightful place helping and interceding with powers granted her by Jesus, her Divine Son.

Her complete protection during dangerous situations; her inspiring hope when events seem hopeless; her protective refuge when trying situations appeared, and her unending blessings showered upon us, hallmark her true identity as our spiritual Mother, the Mother of God.

O Mary, Mother of God, help us to be obedient children of God.

JOHN JULIUS FISHER

□ 26 □

Our Lady of Meliapour — East Indies

Mary gave God the sense to enjoy the perfume of the summer air; to catch the stimulating breeze off the Sea of Galilee; to relish the fragrance of the harvest as He pleaded for more workers in the vineyard. Because of Mary, God, in human form, could experience the odors of the hovels and sympathize with the dwellers of the city canyons. It was through this sense of smell that Christ could know, first hand, the fetid stench of the ulcerous sick that dogged His steps. He responded with many a cure.

It was this example of Christ that inspired the medical missionary to treat the wretched lepers. When someone jeered, "I wouldn't do that for a million dollars," she replied, "Neither would I. But Christ did it, so can I."

The manner in which God used His sense of smell, received from Mary, can motivate us to nurse the indigent sick, aged, and dying with tenderness, understanding, and no signs of revulsion.

O Mary, cause of our joy, pray for us.

ALBERT J. NIMETH, O.F.M.

□ 27 □

Our Lady of Perpetual Help

To expect to have our prayers answered as soon as we make our wishes known is almost to reduce the Almighty (if we dare say it) to the level of a Divine Bell-Boy who is ever ready to jump front and center. Therefore it is important to remember when we get on our knees that we are not rising in our majesty and delivering a command. After all, God is the Creator, and we are only creatures. . .meaning that once we were nothing. The Creator does have all power and can do anything; but it behooves creatures to have all patience, or at least a thimbleful.

Ask our Lady for patience, patience which helps a man plod the roughest road; patience, the cool water that will sprinkle down even flaming anger; patience, the quiet path to peace of heart; patience, the uplifted, admonishing finger of God.

When things go our way, we are happy, but when they do not we can still be contented. Then, things are going God's way.

Have we fully understood the strength, power, and comfort of the Holy Name of Mary?

JOSEPH E. MANTON, C.SS.R.

□ 28 □

Dedication of Notre Dame de Paris — 1325

There is a tradition among the students at Notre Dame University that everyday they make a visit to Our Lady's Grotto.

Mary is a thousand times more anxious to visit us. She proved this at Lourdes, Fatima, and Guadalupe. Everyday we can keep an appointment with Mary by saying her Rosary. We don't have to go down to a grotto to visit our Lady. The very instant we take up her Rosary she will be there to assist us because "never was it known that anyone who fled to thy protection, implored thy help or sought thy intercession was left unaided."

Mary, our Queen, will never let us down.

O Mary, conceived without sin, pray for us who have recourse to thee.

REV. MSGR. HARRY J. WELP

□ 29 □

Our Lady of Buglose — Acqs, Gascony

Artists throughout the Christian ages have impressed Mary upon our minds by their creations as eternally young — the Madonna with an infant in her arms, or with young Jesus at her side.

However, Jesus did grow up and the years laid their aging hands upon Mary as they have done on everyone who has ever lived. No matter what age we may happen to be up to the traditional seventy-two or seventy-four, Mary was once "our age." Scripture does not state that she was spared the ills which afflict us all. She may have had arthritis in her hands, or feet. She nursed Joseph during his infirmities until he died. Then she was a widow. She lost a Son, saw Him falsely accused and His life claimed by the state.

Mary takes on a new dimension when we view her like this: a friend who listens to our trials when others don't; who knows our weaknesses — and understands.

Queen of Peace, pray for us.

ANNE TANSEY

□ 30 □

Our Lady of Calais — Built by the English in France

If all the facts could be written about the blessings which have come to mankind through the centuries as a result of the Rosary, many libraries would have to be devoted exclusively to such writings. God alone knows what to us are the countless extraordinary favors given to those who implored Mary's help through the Rosary — as well as the heresies overcome, wars won, diseases conquered.

Not a day passes by — in fact, not even an hour — when special blessings are not being bestowed upon individuals who are praying their rosaries to seek needed assistance from our Blessed Mother.

The Rosary — embracing as it does the Apostles Creed, the Our Father, the Hail Mary with its angelic salutation and the request for the continued prayer of the Blessed Mother of one's needs now and at the hour of death, and the Glory Be to the Three Persons of the Trinity — is packed with the power that moves heaven to right the wrongs on earth.

Queen of the Holy Rosary, pray for us.

REV. MSGR. RALPH G. KUTZ

J U L Y

□ 1 □

Most Precious Blood;
Dedication of Notre Dame Church — Jumieges, France

As our fingers slip over the beads of the Rosary, we come to the Fourth Sorrowful Mystery — the Carrying of the Cross. The scene is agony compounded for Mary. Exhausted by lack of sleep, wracked by anxiety and concern, she now meets Jesus face to face as He drags His cross to Golgotha.

His sacred face is bruised and caked with blood. He can only communicate with His eyes. And with those eyes He invites His Mother to join Him in the redemption of mankind. Then the soldiers push Him on, and Mary hastens to keep up with her Son.

No human cross can ever be as heavy as the one that Jesus and Mary shared. When the cross falls on you, raise your eyes, as Jesus did, to Mary. The cross will be easier for you, and for others, if your mother helps you.

A Marian Prayer: Mary, holy virgin mother,. . .

EDWIN R. MC DEVITT, M.M.

□ 2 □

Visitation is a good summer word because the summer season spurs visits with families and friends. Just as Mary brought Christ with her when she visited her cousin Elizabeth, then too we also must bring joy to loved ones when we spend some time with them.

Very few of us can speak words as inspired as Mary's *Magnificat* on these occasions. However, whatever we say should reveal our joy to be in touch with other people, who, like ourselves, may often long for friendship, love, and companionship.

Even though Mary had Christ within herself, it was not until she came in contact with Elizabeth that her joy reached its highest level and expression. Read the *Magnificat* today and discover the happiness that results from a genuine contact both with God and with our fellowman.

. . .with love you became the mother of Jesus Christ.

REV. JAMES A. CLARK

□ 3 □

Our Lady of La Carolle — Paris

There are seven instances recorded in Scripture when Mary speaks. She spoke twice to the Archangel: "How shall this be done, since I know not man?" And then, "Behold the handmaid of the Lord. Be it done to me according to thy word." She spoke twice also to her cousin Elizabeth; first to salute her, then to intone the *Magnificat.*

She spoke twice also to her Son; once in the Temple when she said, "Son, why hast Thou done so to us? Behold, Thy father and I have sought Thee, sorrowing." Again at the marriage feast of Cana, she said to Him simply, "They have no wine." Finally, her last word was to the waiters, "Whatsoever He shall say to you, do ye!" And these are the words we should remember.

You gave birth to him, nursed him,

JOSEPH E. MANTON, C.SS.R.

□ 4 □

Our Lady, Refuge of Sinners

Jesus hung for three hours. During this time He prayed for His murderers, promised paradise to the penitent robber, and committed His Blessed Mother to the guardianship of St. John. Then all was finished, and He bowed His head and gave up His spirit.

The worst is over. The holiest is dead and departed. The most tender, the most affectionate, the holiest of the sons of men is gone. Jesus is dead, and with His death my sins shall die. I protest once for all, before men and angels, that sin shall no more have dominion over me.

I promise You, O Lord, with the help of Your grace, to keep out of the way of temptation, to avoid all occasions of sin, to turn at once from the voice of the evil one, to be regular in my prayers, so to die to sin that You may not have died for me on the cross in vain.

. . .and helped him grow to manhood.

REV. WILFRED ILLIES

□ 5 □

Our Lady of Cambrai — Arras, France

Among the treasures of Catholic devotion is certainly the Angelus. This practice of commemorating the Incarnation morning, noon, and evening, and thus honoring the Savior and His Blessed Mother, can be traced to the Middle Ages. References to it in literature and art have been abundant.

In his book on *Ireland*, H.V. Morton, a non-Catholic, describes the profound impression made upon him one day on a crowded bus in Dublin, as suddenly at noon a hush fell, heads bowed, and lips began to move silently. He insists that no one could fail to be impressed by this public display of living faith.

If we pause at the appointed time each day to relive, as it were, the Annunciation, greeting Jesus and Mary, it will take us away from the busy world about us just long enough to deepen our spiritual life, and to gain a great blessing.

With love I return him to you,

MOST REV. JOSEPH M. MARLING, C.PP.S.

□ 6 □

Our Lady of Iron — Blois, France

For Cardinal Merry del Val, Secretary of State to Pope (St.) Pius X, devotion to the Blessed Virgin meant getting closer and closer to Christ by knowing and loving Him better with each passing day. Time and again he would say: "Have great devotion to the Blessed Virgin because the more you have of it the closer you will get to our Blessed Lord. It is impossible to have devotion to the Blessed Virgin without loving our Lord more."

One of his more frequent aspirations was the following: "O Mary, my Mother, how I love thee! Thou teachest me all that I have to know and all that really matters to me, for thou teachest me what Jesus is for me, and what I ought to be for Him."—Dal-Gal, *Spiritual Life of Cardinal Merry del Val.*

How easy is devotion to our Lady if we but remember that she is a Mother, our Mother! One does not have to learn love for a Mother. Mary never fails us. It is rather we who fail her. Humbly ask her to show us the way of love and almost immediately you will notice a difference.

. . .to hold once more,

MOST REV. JOHN J. CARBERRY

□ 7 □

Russia Consecrated to the Immaculate Heart of Mary — 1952

Today, many Catholics look to Mary as the chief foe of communism. Why should the gentlest of all women be regarded as a militant protagonist in a great struggle? That's the way she has been pictured since the day of revelation. "I will put enmities between thee and the woman. . . and thou shalt lie in wait for her heel."

In the Middle Ages Mary was often the Lady to whom the battle was dedicated. Still today, in our disenchanted and effete world, she is a rallying point.

The gentlest of women sounds the call to arms. Her bastion is impregnable; her victory assured. Those who fight under her banner cannot lose. The force of her "fiat" still opposes all who would use the world for their own purposes. The world belongs to her Son.

. . .*to love with all your heart,*

REV. MSGR. J. WILLIAM MC KUNE

□ 8 □

Madonna of Kazan — Russia

Neighborliness is always in place for the Christian, but in these days of prayer and ecumenism, our neighborliness toward our Oriental brothers in Christ is more urgent.

The great saints of the East are our saints too: Athanasius, Basil, the Cyrils, the Damascene, and Ephrem. We are their children; we call them our Fathers. We have one Faith, one Eucharistic Table, one Church. The East should see how we love, honor, and celebrate them!

St. Ephrem's great devotion to Mary should make him a great favorite in our Marian Century. We are sorry not to hear more of the hymns of the "harp of the Holy Spirit," as St. Ephrem is called.

. . .*and to offer to the Holy Trinity*

CONRAD LOUIS, O.S.B.

□ 9 □

Our Lady of Atonement (Society of the Atonement);
Prodigies of Our Lady

May I share a gift with you? Father Paul of Graymoor is my religious father and founder. One of his greatest legacies was the distinctive title and devotion to the Blessed Virgin as Our Lady of the Atonement.

Today is the feast of Our Atonement Mother. It is not a universal feast in the Church but it has the blessing of Rome for the Society of the Atonement and its associates. It honors Mary as co-partner with Christ in the mystery of Salvation; it salutes her as patroness of Christian Unity. She is Our Lady of the At-one-ment.

Jesus prayed "that all may be one." This is the prayer of our Lady too, for she longs to unite all men in the one fold of her Son, the

Church. Pray to Mary for the cause of unity. "There is no surer or easier way of uniting men with Christ than Mary" — St. Pius X.

. . .on our behalf, for your honor

TITUS CRANNY, S.A.

□ 10 □

Our Lady of Boulogne — France

Every woman, married or single, is expected to be the reflection of the lofty virtues of the Mother of God, in every stage and circumstance. It means that she must be upright and pure in sentiment and action; tender, affectionate, and understanding to her husband; diligent, watchful, and wise as mother to her children; able administrator of the home; exemplary citizen of this beloved country, and loyal daughter of the Church. In this a woman reflects her Model.

Help us, O dearly beloved Mother, to respect the duties of our station in life and to make our homes centers of the spiritual life, and of real charity; formative schools of conscience and a garden of all virtues. Bless our intentions and our labors so that always inspired by you in undertaking all that we do, we may restore to the world in ourselves, the ideal and the dignity of the Christian woman and be granted the joy of a truly Christian home.

. . .and for the good of all

G. JOSEPH GUSTAFSON, S.S.

□ 11 □

Our Lady of Clery — France

Mary was not singled out merely as the natural vehicle by which the natural body of Christ was to come into the world. The purpose of the Incarnation being supernatural — the reclaiming of man from sin and giving of life to him in Christ — the office of Mary must be correspondingly supernatural. So we can say that by consenting to the mystery of the Incarnation Mary became our Spiritual Mother.

By bringing into the world the body of Christ to which we mystically belong, her motherhood of man is renewed and confirmed. By uniting herself with her Son's redemptive act on Good Friday, her spiritual motherhood in our regard is finally ratified.

Since it is on Calvary that Christ brought His work for man to its climax, it is on Calvary that Mary's spiritual motherhood of man is crowned. Our Lord's *"consummatum est"* speaks for His mother's sacrifices as well as His own. As she has shared His work, . . . so now she shares . . . the last act and fulfillment. — Dom Hubert Van Zeller, O.S.B., *The Inner Search.*

. . .your pilgrim sons and daughters

MOST REV. LEO A. PURSLEY

□ 12 □

Our Lady of All Graces

The heart has long been a symbol of love. No heart of any human person can symbolize immense love as does the Immaculate Heart of the Blessed Virgin Mary. All human beings are her children and she is interested in the well-being of each of them.

Although countless are the afflictions that beset human beings, still more countless are the helps given by our Blessed Mother through her Immaculate Heart. Whether it be poverty and need or an unhealthy body on a bed of sickness or a soul steeped in sin or any other type of affliction sufferable by a person, the Heart of Mary goes out to bring comfort, consolation, and peace.

Designated as the mediatrix of all grace, our Blessed Mother through her Immaculate Heart will never leave unaided those who flee to her protection, implore her help, or seek her intercession. As St. Bernard well advises: "Go to Mary."

. . .in this world.

REV. MSGR. RALPH G. KUTZ

□ 13 □

Our Lady of Chartres

"And when the Spirit comes, He will teach you all things." But who will learn? Learning requires listening — being attentive. Without alert attention, lessons are lost. The atmosphere of listening cannot be captured in a moment. It grows and develops through preparation.

We are told that our Lady and the Apostles and disciples prepared themselves by prayer and recollection for nine days before the Holy Spirit came. They were then ready to hear and respond to Him.

Some persons are the "gimme" type in their communication with God. They turn to Him only when they need something and they want it in a hurry. Their inability to unite with God because of the absence of living with Him makes their prayers devoid of His Spirit.

Lord, let me be aware of and listen to Your Spirit at all times.

Mother, . . .

THERESITA POLZIN

□ 14 □

St. Bonaventure;
Our Lady of the Bush — Portugal

St. Bonaventure was a thirteenth-century theologian. He was given the name of "Seraphic Doctor" and he well deserved it. His spiritual writings were as mighty and effective as his theological treatises. He was a Franciscan and he taught theology and Scripture in Paris from 1248 until 1257. At that time he became General of his Order and did much to give a definitive rule to his community as well as to encourage study about the Blessed Virgin and promote devotion to her.

In 1273, he was made Bishop of Albano and a cardinal, mainly for the purpose of doing what he could to end the schism between the Western and the Eastern Church.

When he died, July 14, 1274, he felt an agreement had at last been reached, but we know how short-lived it really was. He was deservedly listed with the saints by Pope Sixtus IX.

. . .pray to God for me,

JOHN C. SELNER, S.S.

□ 15 □

Bouillon Defeats Turks (Through Mary's Intercession)

"Say the Rosary with attention to the mysteries. Consecration to the Immaculate Heart of Mary. Communions and reparation on the First Saturdays. Sanctification of our daily duties."

This message is not something new, nor a revelation or prophecy. Pope John XXIII in his message to Americans urged consecration to Mary and added: "Mary cannot be completely and perfectly honored unless we carry on our fight with courage by her side."

This fight for souls, between Mary and Satan, has been going on for two thousand years! Suffering plays an important role in the salvation of souls. God helps by sending crosses. The Cross of Jesus was caused by the ignorance, stupidity, and malice of men.

The cross prepared for you by the ignorance, stupidity, and malice of others is the most meritorious and has the greatest redemptive power. "Beyond the Cross is the crown."

. . .for the forgiveness of my sins,

MOST REV. REMBERT KOWALSKI, O.F.M. (China)

□ 16 □

Our Lady of Mount Carmel;
Last Apparition at Lourdes — 1858

St. Simon Stock, Minister General of the Carmelite Order, appealed to our Lady for her protection of his Order. On this day in 1251 the Blessed Mother appeared to him at Cambridge, England, and presented him with the Brown Scapular that became the prototype of all other scapulars.

Bishop St. Germain spoke of our Lady on the feast of the Presentation:

"Hail Mary, full of grace, holier than the Saints, higher than the Heavens, more glorious than the Cherubim, more honorable than the Seraphim, to be reverenced above every creature. Hail, holy and immaculate building, most pure palace of God, adorned with the magnificence of the Divine King. Hail holy throne of God, divine treasury, house of glory, chosen and sacred mercy-seat for the whole world. O Virgin most pure who brought forth a Son, and Mother who knew no man, hidden treasure of innocence and holiness. By your prayers to your Son direct all those who govern the life of the Church and lead us to the harbor of peace."

. . .for the grace I need

REV. MSGR. JOHN J. DUGGAN

JULY

□ 17 □

Humility of Our Lady

Years ago I was privileged to be on Mount Carmel, in Israel, and to visit the birthplace of the Carmelites. . . . Yes, I bought scapulars there. I have been wearing the medal, though, for years.

The Scapular was the sign God gave St. Simon Stock, through the hands of Mary, of the protection He would give those who revered His Mother.

Clothes are the symbol of the person. Like the Christian heart, dress must be chaste and simple. Don't we usually judge the interior by the exterior? The Scapular should remind us that we have an apostolate against current extremes and extravagances in modes of dress.

. . .to serve him more faithfully.

REV. MSGR. DAVID P. SPELGATTI

□ 18 □

Our Lady of Victory — Toledo, Spain

"Inasmuch as the enemies of Christianity are so stubborn in their aims, its defenders must be equally staunch, especially as the heavenly help and the benefits which are bestowed on us by God are more usually the fruits of our perseverance."

These are again prophetic words of Leo XIII. How accurately Pope Leo analyzed the spirit of those who are opposed to Christianity. They have one object: to destroy Christianity, to destroy morality, to blot out religion and all that it teaches. Nothing is an obstacle, they never rest.

The defenders of Christianity must prepare for battle. The Rosary is our special weapon. If we look at the Rosary it is seen as more than a private devotion — it becomes a source of strength against the forces of paganism.

May it please God that all will know the Rosary and love the Rosary and say the Rosary daily.

. . .Pray that I may be true to Christ

MOST REV. JOHN J. CARBERRY

□ 19 □

Our Lady of Moyen-Pont — Peronne, France

Mary was the person closest to Christ on earth, and she is even closer to Him now in heaven. For thirty years in their little cottage at Nazareth she saw Him and cared for Him and conversed with Him. No one knows Jesus better than she. No wonder, then, we turn to her and ask her to intercede for us, and we know she will.

Sin had no part in Mary. She showed what God can do with human nature, if one has an open heart. Mary was the first to be clothed in sanctity. She was the first Christian and she is the best Christian. Most wondrous of all, Jesus in His kindness gave Mary to us to be our Mother. So now we are doubly blessed. We have a good Mother here on earth, and we have a beautiful Mother in heaven as well, to look after us.

Mary is grace and smiling light. Cardinal John Henry Newman said, "She exerts a gentle sway over our hearts."

. . .until the moment of my death,

REV. RAWLEY MYERS

□ 20 □

Our Lady of Grace

Mary is a Mother to us in the order of grace.

"This maternity . . . began with the consent which she gave in faith at the Annunciation and which she sustained without wavering beneath the cross. This maternity will last without interruption until the eternal fulfillment of all the elect. For, taken up to heaven, she did not lay aside this saving role, but by her manifold acts of intercession continues to win for us gifts of eternal salvation.

"By her maternal charity, Mary cares for the brethren of her Son who still journey on earth surrounded by dangers and difficulties, until they are led to their happy fatherland. Therefore the Blessed Virgin is invoked by the Church under the titles of Advocate, Auxiliatrix, Adjutrix, and Mediatrix," always subordinate and with reference to her Son — *Dogmatic Constitution on the Church*, Nos. 61, 62.

. . .so that I may come to praise him with you,

FELICIAN A. FOY, O.F.M.

□ 21 □

Our Lady of Verdun — Lorraine

In the words of the psalmist, God's whisper came to Mary: "Hearken, O daughter, and see, and incline thine ear; and forget thy people, and thy father's house; and the King shall greatly covet thy beauty." She made God's will her own. With extreme joy, in the words of Holy David, Mary said: "I rejoiced at the things that were said to me: we shall go into the house of the Lord."

Mary prostrated herself in adoration of the Divine Majesty. She presented and offered herself for His perpetual service. She made the resolution to serve Him forever, all her life, in His Holy Temple. God had greater things for her, at Bethlehem, Nazareth, and elsewhere. He was pleased with Mary's offering. He accepted it with great pleasure.

"Behold me here, O Lord. I am come into Thy house to be Thy slave forever. Receive me into Thy service: for I desire no more glorious lot than to serve Thee." In her heart, God made answer to this: "Let My Beloved come into My garden, O My sister, My spouse."

. . . *forever and ever. Amen.*

MARIE LAYNE

□ 22 □

Our Lady of Safety — Marseilles, France

The serpent was right. Man's first sin did give him knowledge of good and evil. The man and the woman saw that God was Perfect Good and that they were nothing — poor, naked creatures utterly dependent on the God they had challenged. Ashamed and frightened they sought a cover-up.

The woman at the dawn of time persuaded man to try the way of human independence and self-praise — a muddy track full of snags and pitfalls leading down into wilderness.

In the fullness of time, another woman withdrew all claim to live her own life and responded to God in complete faith and love. Clothed in His splendor she began to walk back up the mountain that led to God in perfect freedom, bearing within her the hope of all men — Life itself.

Like a clear pool, completely receptive to God, Mary let His glory be made manifest in her, become incarnate in her and through her to glorify all men and the whole of creation.

A Marian Prayer: Mother of mercy and love,

ANNE O'NEILL

□ 23 □

*Order of Prémontré Instituted
Through Revelation of Our Lady*

Who knows better than Jesus the importance of the home? As Nazareth was the starting point of the Redemption, so today the Christian home is the cradle of virtues, the foundation of the Church and the State.

It is no wonder then, we have these promises: "I will bless every home in which the image of My Heart shall be exposed and honored. I will give them all the graces necessary for their state of life. I will establish peace in their families."

Dear Sacred Heart, my King and my Friend, according to Your request, the image of Your Sacred Heart is honored in my home. It reminds me of Your love for me in the Blessed Sacrament. Frequent Mass and Communion will bring Your blessings to my home. Grant them to me, through the Immaculate Heart of Mary, Queen of Peace. Amen.

. . .blessed Virgin Mary,

FRANCIS LARKIN, SS.CC.

□ 24 □

Our Lady of Cambron — France

God's ways are not the same as ours. In fact, His plans are often directly the opposite of the way we are used to doing things. That is why faith is essential to our relationship with God. Faith is accepting what God says, even if it seems unlikely.

Mary is the perfect example of a woman of faith. When the angel told her she would bear the Messiah, she didn't say, "Well, it doesn't seem too likely that God would choose me." She said, "Let it be done to me as you have said." Mary trusted the Lord's word to her, and Elizabeth proclaims her "blest" because of that trust.

God's word to us seems equally unlikely: He loves us, He accepts us, He longs for us to come to Him. That is the word proclaimed at every Mass we attend. May we hear with hearts of faith, and trust, as Mary did, that His word to us will be fulfilled.

. . .I am a poor and unworthy sinner,

CHRISTINE DUBOIS

□ 25 □

Our Lady of La Bouchet — France

T hose of us who are older remember the words of the song so very well: "Mary, it's a grand old name."

There is no doubt that we learned our catechism lesson very well — you have to choose at least one saint's name at the time of baptism and another for confirmation; so the Christian person can have someone special to imitate. But do we remember this when we are choosing a name, especially for a baby? More often, it becomes a matter of which relative is going to be honored or choosing a first name that goes well with the last and then hoping there is a saint by this name.

Years ago, I read that those of us who are named *John* have eighty-seven patrons, indicating that we are a very illustrious group or that we need more help than anyone else.

Are you acquainted with the life of your patron saint? If not, why not try to find out about it today?

. . .and I turn to you

REV. JOHN R. MAGUIRE

□ 26 □

Our Lady of Faith;
St. Anne, Mother of Our Lady;
Our Lady, Help of Those in Their Last Agony

I t is natural that the Catholic heart is drawn in warm affection to the good woman whom God chose to be the mother of the Mother of His Son. Good children resemble in significant ways their good parents; we may be sure that some of the lovely traits of Mary were a more brilliant reflection of the same virtues in her beloved mother. We have no strict facts about St. Anne except this one — that she is our Lady's mother. It is enough.

It is natural also that Catholic devotion should repose special confidence in the intercessory power of good St. Anne. The relationship of St. Anne to Mary and Jesus is a matter of blood and family, and such ties are strong. One feels that it is hardly possible for the Lord Christ to refuse a loving request which comes both from His Mother and from His *Bonne* — as the French wisely call a grandmother.

. . . in confidence and love.

VINCENT P. MC CORRY, S.J.

□ 27 □

Miraculous Defeat of the Turks
in 1840 Through Help of Our Lady

St. Cyril was Mary's champion against the heretic Nestorius in the fourth century; he had attacked the incarnation of Christ and the divine motherhood of the Blessed Virgin Mary. The doctrine of St. Cyril was upheld in the Council of Ephesus, proclaiming Mary as the Mother of God.

The Second Vatican Council has referred to the Council of Ephesus and how the devotion of Christians to the Mother of God has wonderfully increased in veneration and love, in invocation and imitation, according to her own prophetic words, "All generations shall call me blessed, because He that is mighty has done great things to me"— Luke 1.48.

You stood by your Son,

PASCHAL BOLAND, O.S.B.

□ 28 □

Our Lady of Smolensk — Russia

Can you picture yourself as a prisoner of the Chinese communists, placed in solitary confinement, with a guard watching over you twenty-four hours a day? You have no Rosary and you want to pray to Mary. The mind is too weary and it is difficult to keep track of the prayers.

Suddenly you notice five or six burnt safety matches in your cell. By breaking these matches you are now able to keep track of the prayers of the Rosary. The guards think you are crazy and this is one of the reasons you are not put to death.

This happened to Father Robert Greene, M.M., who lived to tell us in his book, *Calvary in China,* of his devotion to the Rosary and how it saved his life. May it please God for us to pray the Rosary daily.

. . .*as he hung dying on the cross.*

MOST. REV. JOHN J. CARBERRY

□ 29 □

Decrees Related to Immaculate Conception Confirmed at Council of Trent, 1545-1563

In Mary, the Virgin Mother, the Church has reached that perfection whereby she exists "holy and immaculate, without stain or wrinkle or anything of that sort" — Ephesians 5.27. The rest of mankind must strive for that perfection by conquering sin and growing in the life and love of God.

For inspiration and help in our continual struggle upward we are urged to look at Mary. She stands as an ideal and mirrors in her life the Church and the truths the Church professes.

The Council Fathers never intended to minimize devotion to Mary. They called upon all the faithful to promote and respect the age-old devotional practices, updated to suit modern times. They called on teachers to study the Bible, the Fathers of the Church, and the authentic teaching of the Church in order to avoid false exaggerations on the one hand and too narrow a view on the other. Virtue lies in the middle.

Stand by me also, a poor sinner, and by all the members of the Church.

ALBERT J. NIMETH, O.F.M.

□ 30 □

Our Lady of Gray — Besancon, France

Candles are symbols of the lovers of Christ. The candle gives light, but the heat of the light consumes the candle entirely. The human "candle" which loves Christ lights the way to Him for others, but burns while it does so.

There is not much use for candles these days except to burn near a tabernacle — during Holy Mass mainly. Did you ever think of yourself at Mass as a burning candle? And does the flame burn brightly long after you get home?

Yes, there is light too. When Simeon in the spirit of prophecy held the Child Jesus to his heart and Mary looked on, he raised his dim, aged eyes to heaven and called our Lord "a revelation to the Gentiles." Light indeed! The Light of the world! And you should be a bright spark of that light. But don't forget, the Light that is Christ shoots forth over the centuries from a burning furnace of love!

Pray that we may be worthy followers of our Lord and Savior, Jesus Christ,

JOHN C. SELNER, S.S.

□ 31 □

Our Lady of the Slain — Ceica, Portugal

For three hours Jesus hangs on the Cross in pain. Three hours His Mother stands at the Cross erect, not swooning, but in contemplation of the Victim — her Son — hanging there; helpless to help Him! She unites with that bloody Sacrifice of Jesus, the agony of her bleeding heart. The sacrifice of Jesus was complete. He had given us His Body and Blood and all He had in this world; and now He will give even His Mother away. "Woman, behold thy son." After that He said to John: "Behold thy Mother."

John represented us. What an exchange! After we had offended Him and helped to nail Him to the Cross, He gives us His Mother to be our Mother, so that He could be our Brother on His Mother's side!

And Mary accepts us as "her eyes bleed tears and His wounds weep blood." O Mother, be to me what thou were to the beloved disciple. Like him, take me to thy own.

. . . in the sight of the most holy Trinity, our most high God. Amen.

MOST REV. REMBERT KOWALSKI, O.F.M. (China)

AUGUST

□ 1 □

Our Lady of Victory — Russia

When a distinguished visitor to the Vatican asked Pope Pius XI what was the most valuable treasure there, the Pope drew from his pocket a well-worn rosary, pointed to it, and said, "This is the greatest treasure anywhere."

At Lourdes, our Lady appeared some eighteen times and invited Bernadette to say the Rosary with her. In the six appearances at Fatima, our Lady insisted on the recitation of the Rosary.

At Fatima, Mary identified herself, saying "I am the Lady of the Rosary, and I have come to warn the faithful to amend their lives and ask pardon for their sins. . . . They must say the Rosary."

Through the Rosary today, as in past times of peril that have threatened civilization, Mary has again come to save men from the evils that overwhelm them.

The Angelic Salutation: Hail, Mary, full of grace,

REV. MSGR. CHARLES HUGO DOYLE

□ 2 □

In the Old Testament we read of an angel, to whom Isaiah does not even give a name, who killed 185,000 Assyrian soldiers one night to protect King David.

The Blessed Virgin Mary, however, is so much greater and more powerful than all the angels, archangels, all the created members of the human race, past, present, and future, that there can be no comparison.

Yet she is not divine. She is one of us, the real heavenly Mother of us all, appointed so by her Divine Son. "It has never been known that anyone who fled to her protection was left unaided." At the moment of death she is to be our advocate.

She is the Queen of Heaven. The Archangel Michael will gaze upon her for eternity with increasing admiration. Should we ever tire to pray to her, beg her protection, sing her praises, in life and in the dread hour of death when her Divine Son pronounces the irrevocable judgment?

. . . *the Lord is with you.*

TOM MARTIN, S.J.

□ 3 □

Our Lady of Bows — London

The direct meaning of our Lord's two brief sentences — *Woman, behold thy son: Behold thy mother* — was that He entrusted His Mother to His best-beloved disciple as a sacred charge. . . . To some it has seemed arbitrary to say more than that, or even as much. But, if we revert to the great principle of the Mystical Body of Christ and to our incorporation with Him, we see that we are driven to say much more! For in that Mystical Body Mary too exists. And within it, she holds a position that is not ours and cannot be. She is the Mother of Christ. Therefore she is the Mother of the whole Christ, in whom are we, incorporate.

You cannot, as it were, detach and departmentalize Mary, and make her exclusively Mother of Christ insofar as He lived at Nazareth or sojourned in Palestine. She is, altogether and always, what at any time and in any way she was. — Rev. C. C. Martindale, S.J.

. . .*Blessed are you among women,*

VINCENT P. MC CORRY, S.J.

□ 4 □

Madonna of Dordrecht — Holland

Today was formerly the feast of St. Dominic. He had much to do with the Rosary and it has become the favorite form of devotion to the Blessed Virgin. There are so many indulgences attached to the Rosary that they can hardly be enumerated. To gain them we must meditate on the fifteen mysteries at least five at a time. If our lives are supposed to be brought into conformity with the life of Christ — and the mysteries of the Rosary give us the outstanding events of His life — it should follow that they will also be the milestones in our own.

The Agony in the Garden represents the indecision we frequently have in embracing the life of Christ in a particular instance. The Crowning with Thorns is the subjection of our rational nature whose pride so frequently had led us astray. The Scourging at the Pillar to give us control over the flesh. The Carrying of the Cross, the gift of final perseverance. The Crucifixion represents the complete giving of our lives to God.

The Rosary takes on a new meaning when we attach it to our own lives.

. . .*and blessed is the fruit of your womb, Jesus.*

REV. MSGR. JOSEPH B. LUX

□ 5 □

Our Lady of the Snows

One of the earth's testimonials of love for the Blessed Virgin Mary is that basilica in Rome called St. Mary Major. It was built on a spot on the Esquiline Hill, as legend tells, which Mary herself designated to Pope Sixtus III by a snowfall during August, in the year 350.

The legend is not nearly so remarkable as the fact of the divine maternity which this temple honors. We need no summer snowfall to make us marvel at the mystery which the Church recounts in the liturgical hymn sung this day:

"The womb of Mary bears Him who rules the threefold fabric of the universe, whom the earth, the sea and the stars honor, worship and proclaim." Whatever we venerate in Mary is venerable because it is of God and because it represents what God has given to our humanity.

Holy Mary, mother of God,

MOST REV. THOMAS K. GORMAN

□ 6 □

Our Lady of Capacavana — Bolivia

The best example of a person of prayer is the woman, Mary! She is the delight in the eyes of God. At a very early age she gave herself most completely and most honestly into His love. The vocation to which Mary was called was not only awesome and sublime and beautiful. It was also frightening, terrible, and (at the moment) embarrassing. And yet Mary loved. She was faith-filled. She was a pray-er, and her prayer was: "I am the handservant of the Lord! Let it be done to me as you say." How great her love, her faith, her prayer!

I remember that as a child my mother taught me the poem: "Lovely Lady, dressed in blue, teach me how to pray. God was just your little boy, and you know the way." It is only now that I more fully realize not just the beauty but also the truth of the poem. The truth that Mary is the model pray-er.

. . .pray for us sinners,

REV. T. TIMOTHY DELANEY

□ 7 □

Our Lady of Schiedem — Holland

"Be with us, O Mary, who are your children. Guide us along the path which leads to God." This is our prayer to our heavenly Mother.

We know that in praying thus, she will not fail us. For no one was closer to Christ than she. Mary was the nurse of His helpless infancy, the teacher of His youth. And she is now our Mother, the Mother of all living, the hope for the weak, the refuge of sinners, the comforter of the afflicted. We kiss the hem of her garment and kneel in the shadow of her throne. For she is full of grace and glory, our Lady, our Mother, the Blessed Virgin Mary.

"She is not like earthly beauty," a saintly soul wrote, "but like the morning star, infusing peace in the dark night."

. . .*now and at the hour of our death. Amen.*

REV. RAWLEY MYERS

□ 8 □

Notre Dame de la Kuen — near Brussels

Mary of Nazareth never knew moral evil. But what is most touching about the sinlessness of Mary is her mother's compassion for the soiled, sad human being who is steeped in sin. *Holy Virgin of Virgins*, we cry to our Lady in her Litany, *Mother Most Pure, Mother Most Chaste, Mother Inviolate, Mother Undefiled, Mirror of Justice, Tower of Ivory, House of God;* and then: *Refuge of Sinners.*

It is a strange thing, Christian man and woman, that the Immaculate Mother of God should have a care for you or me. But she has. In all our misery she pities and loves us, like the true, good Mother that she is. She will not give over until, in every sense, she has brought us to her Son.

Thus we pray in one of the best-loved Marian prayers: "And after this our exile show unto us the blessed fruit of thy womb."

The Hail, Holy Queen: Hail, Holy Queen,. . .

VINCENT P. MC CORRY, S.J.

□ 9 □

Our Lady of Oegnies — Brabant, France

We honor Mary as the Mother of Jesus Christ, the Incarnate Word of God. We recognize her unique and exalted role in the redemption her Son brought to men. Because we love Mary, we strive to imitate her virtues of faith, purity, humility and conformity to the will of God.

AUGUST

The more we know and love Mary, the more surely will we know and love her Son and better understand His mission in the world. The more we know and love Jesus, the better we shall appreciate His Mother's place in God's plan for the redemption of man.

Mary, the Mother of God, is called by many titles because she is the universal patron of every Christian man, woman, and child who has ever sought to follow more closely the vocation to which they are called by Christ. Relying on the instinct of faith, the devout sum up the truth about Mary in the salutation: "Hail, Holy Queen! Mother of Mercy! Our Life, our Sweetness, and our Hope!"

...*Mother of Mercy:*

THOMAS M. BREW, S.J.

□ **10** □

Our Lady of Mercy;
Our Lady of Ransom — Spain

I'm coming, Lord, grant me a little time —
A little space —
With stumbling haste my way to thee I'll find
By help of grace.
The thought of falling haunts me and makes
My soul afraid.
Unfurl thy wings, O Angel guarding me,
Fly to mine aid!
O, Mother Mary, stoop to succor me whene'er I fall,
And stay forever close that you will hear
My pleading call.
Thou knowest that I seek thy Son alone —
My Love! My Christ!
O Jesus, weary not at my delay, I'll keep Thy tryst.

— Eileen Duffy

...*Hail, our life, our sweetness, and our hope:*

ALBERT A. MURRAY, C.S.P.

□ 11 □

Mary conceived the God-man by the power of the Holy Spirit. Mary's love exceeds the comprehension of both men and angels combined.

What a life of joyful intimacy Jesus and Mary had for nine months! Man could never have thought of it. It is beyond man's imagination. It is more of a wonder than the mystery it is.

Mary was meant to be the "mold" of not only the Son of God but also of all the sons of God! By the power of the Holy Spirit, Mary shapes and forms us until we give birth to Christ in our souls. Nothing delights her more. So much is this true that when we say "Mary," she says "Jesus."

...To you do we cry,

BRUCE RISKI, O.F.M. Cap.

□ 12 □

Notre Dame de Rouen — Normandy

If we truly believe in the Redemption, we have to face a startling fact: any pain which Jesus suffered on this earth was caused by sin. Any consolations He ever had — and there were few of them — came from virtue and love, or from sharing His pain. His Mother comforted Him the most and therefore she suffered the most.

But the Redemption is going on still. Every sin that is ever committed must be expiated, either by the sinner or by someone else in union with Christ. But it was our Lord's sacrifice that made anyone else's worth offering.

His aches, His rebuffs, His weariness, His loneliness, His agonies, His death were our sins — buffeting Him. The greatest pain Christ could know was to have us pulled away from Him: only sin can do that. That is why our Lady runs to the sinner and cries, "Don't!"

...poor banished children of Eve;

JOHN C. SELNER, S.S.

AUGUST

☐ 13 ☐

Our Lady, Refuge of Sinners

Above the golden dome of the main building of Notre Dame stands the statue of our Lady, after whom the university is named. Thousands of students pray daily before her statue in the grotto, a replica of Lourdes.

Mary is the Patron of Youth, the Help of Christians, and the Refuge of Sinners. Pray to her each day to obtain for you the graces needed for your station in life. She will never fail you.

A beautiful custom for every Catholic family to observe is that of reciting, after the evening meal, the Family Rosary. Have each member take the lead in reciting a decade. Meditate carefully upon the mystery commemorated in each of the decades. In this way, the life of Christ and of His Blessed Mother will be kept vividly before your mind. So too will you receive the prayers and intercession of our Blessed Mother.

. . .*to you do we send up our sighs,*

REV. JOHN A. O'BRIEN

☐ 14 ☐

Vigil of the Assumption

The scientific precision with which the Church handles the truths of God's revelation was most evident, November 1, 1950, when Pope Pius XII proclaimed our Lady's Assumption as a dogma of faith. He said that she was "assumed body and soul into heavenly glory *when the course of her earthly life was completed."*

On the eve of the feast of the Assumption we should thank God not only for having triumphantly established our Mother Mary in heaven, but also for having left us our Mother, the Church, here on earth.

. . .*mourning and weeping in this valley of tears.*

REV. FRANCIS R. MOESLEIN

AUGUST

□ 15 □

Assumption of Our Lady

Mary's Assumption is a reminder to each of us that our home is in heaven. We belong there. We have a visa that no one can cancel. As we go our round of duties, with headaches and backaches mingled with laughter and tears, our Heavenly Mother's bodily assumption recalls to our minds that our bodies and souls are destined for immortality. As St. Paul put it: "This corruptible body must put on incorruption, and this mortal body must put on immortality." Mary's glorification in heaven is a promise and a pledge that our bodies, too, will rise glorified with new vigor and vitality undreamed of in this world.

Mary's Assumption brings to us this assurance of Christian hope. Because she has gone before us, we know that our assumption is that much the more certain. By her entrance into our Father's land, she can wait with a mother's eagerness to welcome all her children back to their native land. By being lifted up to heaven, Mary has brought heaven more closely within the reach of every mortal man and woman.

...*Turn, then, most gracious advocate,*

REV. VINCENT A. YZERMANS

□ 16 □

Our Lady of Trapani — Sicily

In the full blaze of the Assumption, the final triumph of Mary, the Church gives us in the liturgy — her father, St. Joachim. We know nothing of Joachim and Anne, the parents of Mary, except what we know of Mary herself.

We know the Holy Family: Jesus, Mary, and Joseph. They are given to us as a model for all Christian families. But perhaps we are inclined to think the model is too difficult for imitation: Jesus is divine, Mary is conceived immaculate, and Joseph is a foster father.

Well here is another holy family more closely fitted to our circumstances: Mary, Anne, and Joachim: a holy, peaceful, and hardworking family, living in the presence of God. Joachim was the grandfather of Jesus. Perhaps our Lord bore a family resemblance to him. Perhaps He

AUGUST

went to stay with His grandparents sometimes. Perhaps He learned the family prayers and the reading of the scriptures from His grandfather.

What the Church in her liturgy says of Joachim, she can say of every man.

. . .*your eyes of mercy toward us;*

MOST REV. THOMAS K. GORMAN

□ 17 □

Madonna of Grace — Mantua

"Mediatrix of All Graces" is a title of Mary that perplexes some people. The Second Vatican Council said this: "The maternal duty of Mary toward men in no wise obscures or diminishes that unique mediation of Christ but rather shows His power. For every saving influence of the Blessed Virgin on men originates, not from her inner necessity but from the divine treasury. It flows from the superabundance of the merits of Christ, rests on His mediation, depends entirely upon it and draws all power from it. It no way impedes but rather fosters the immediate union of the faithful with Christ." The importance of the Incarnation points up the importance and value of the role of Mary. God, no one else, chose Mary as the means of His coming among us.

If it were not for the coming of Christ, there would be no grace. But Christ came through the physical mediation of Mary and through no other means. This fact, coupled with Mary's perfect faith and special union with her risen Son gives her a special kind of mediation. Makes her the Mediatrix of all graces.

. . .*and after this, our exile,*

ALBERT J. NIMETH, O.F.M.

□ 18 □

Coronation of Mary — Central America

At her Immaculate Conception, Mary's soul was endowed with an intense degree of hope; but the full perfection of that hope was crowned in heaven only after a lifetime of trials. Her hope, like all her virtues and perfections, centered around Jesus. Jesus was the object of her Faith — her Baby, her Boy, her Son, was her God! Jesus was the object of her love — her God was her Son!

Jesus was the object of her perfect hope. As she stood near Him on Calvary — He with a lance in His side, she with a sword in her soul — only her boundless trust in God kept her from dying of sorrow.

While there is hope, there is life. Mary was an optimist, even on Calvary, because she saw God's will in everything. Hopeful optimism is a virtue God expects of me.

. . .show unto us

PATRICK PEYTON, C.S.C.

□ 19 □

Our Lady of the Door — Russia;
Holy Heart of Mary

"My heart has exulted in the Lord."

Today we celebrate a feast in honor of the sinless and love-filled heart of our Mother Mary. The heart is a universal symbol, not only of love, but of the whole inner personality and personal life of a human being. A man is "good-hearted," we say, or perhaps he is "hard-hearted."

Mary's heart was constantly loving God, especially in her own Son, Jesus. She was also loving us and suffering for us with Christ. Now she is in heaven and her heart is perfectly filled with divine life. Let us ask her with absolute confidence to pray for us, to care for us, to save every human being. Above all, let us ask her to teach us how to imitate her life and virtues, to have each day a heart more like hers full of kindness and mercy.

. . .the blessed fruit of your womb, Jesus.

SISTER M. CHARLES BORROMEO, C.S.C.

□ 20 □

Commemoration of St. Bernard's "Ave Maria"
and Mary's "Ave Bernarde"

While it is a common practice to seek to improve anything authored by man, there are some things which quite defy such attempts. One such thing that has stood the test of time is the advice given to us by the learned St. Bernard in his tribute to our Blessed Mother.

"The name of Mary, when interpreted, is called 'Star of the Sea,' and is admirably suited to the Virgin Mother. . . .

"O you, who realize that in the rushing tide of this world you are bobbing about amid storms and tempests rather than walking on land, turn not your eyes away from the light of this star if you do not wish to be lost in the storm. If the winds of temptation blow up, if you are running over mountains of tribulations, look up to this star; call on Mary. . . .

"If, when overwhelmed by the immensity of your crimes, when ashamed by the ugliness of your conscience, when frightened by horror for the judgment, you begin to sink into the abyss of despair, think of Mary. . . ."

. . .*O clement, O loving, O sweet Virgin Mary. Amen.*

REV. MSGR. RALPH G. KUTZ

□ 21 □

*Institution of the Order
of the Thirty Knights of Our Lady*

"If the virtuous man turns from the path of virtue to do evil. . .none of his virtuous deeds shall be remembered." God demands love and faithfulness in all things. There is no way of being partly faithful, somewhat loving, sometimes obedient. We cannot follow the Lord off and on. There are no part-time saints.

There is no way to holiness without perseverance. Seven prominent men of Florence joining together to become Servants of Mary had learned that lesson. To persevere in the Lord, to give themselves entirely to the service of God they left homes, work, families, businesses and professions. To escape the visitors who interrupted their prayer and penance they "fled" into the mountain.

Lord, help me be faithful to Your law in all things and do not let me grow weary of doing Your will.

A Marian Prayer: Ave Regina Caelorum. . .

NORMAN PERRY, O.F.M.

AUGUST

☐ 22 ☐

Queenship of Blessed Virgin Mary

The theme of this observance is the same as that of the last mystery of the Rosary, the Crowning of Mary as Queen of heaven and earth, of men and angels. The memorial was decreed by Pope Pius XII in 1954 near the close of a Marian Year marking the centenary of the proclamation of the dogma of the Immaculate Conception. The pope urged:

"Let all strive vigilantly and strenuously to reproduce, each according to his own condition, in their own souls and in their own conduct the exalted virtues of our heavenly Queen and our most loving Mother. And hence it will follow that those who are counted as Christians, honoring and imitating their Queen and Mother, will finally realize that they are truly brothers and, spurning jealousies and immoderate desires, may promote social charity, respect the rights of the weak, and love peace. And let no one consider himself a child of Mary to be taken readily under her most powerful protection unless, according to her example, he practices justice, meekness and chastity, and devotes himself to true brotherhood, not harming or hurting anyone, but rather helping and consoling."

. . .*Hail, Queen of the heavens!*

FELICIAN A. FOY, O.F.M.

☐ 23 ☐

Victory of Philip of Valois over Flemings
in 1328 Through Our Lady's Help

The story of Queen Esther is well known from the Old Testament. Through her powerful intercession with King Assuerus, she was able to plead the cause of the Jewish people and save them from great harm. From the earliest days the Church has proposed Esther as a striking figure of the Virgin Mary.

To fathom Christ's boundless love for His Mother is impossible, but the attempt provides a clue to her ability to obtain graces and favors for us. What a pity if one who loves our Lord does not avail himself of this added help in his struggle to fulfill the divine Will.

To picture Mary as an obstacle between ourselves and Jesus is a distorted view. Her role is not to impede but to quicken the approach to Him. Nor does acknowledgment of her Queenship detract from Christ's Kingship. The one accentuates the other. It is only because Christ is King that Mary is Queen.

...Hail, Empress of the angels!

MOST REV. JOSEPH M. MARLING, C.PP.S.

□ 24 □

Our Lady of Czestochowa — Poland

Many feasts of Mary are remembered throughout the year. Some of these are recalled with greater festivity by special groups. One such festivity is the feast of Our Lady of Czestochowa, the Queen of Poland. Under this title, Mary is also known as the "Black Madonna." The people of Poland have a great devotion to Mary under this title of Our Lady of Czestochowa.

The story is related that St. Luke painted this picture of Mary on the top of a cypress table. It was transported to Poland many years later during the time of the Tartars. In the picture the two scars on our Lady's cheek are reportedly due to the slashes of the sword of a soldier who fell dead before a third slash could be made.

It has been advocated that true devotion to Mary leads to a greater closeness to her Son. May our love and devotion to Mary be our guide to Jesus.

...Hail, the source...the gate...

SISTER MARY MAUREEN, S.S.J.

□ 25 □

Our Lady of Monte Berico — Vicenza

Besides being a great saint, Mary was a mother, with the very same love for and pride in her Son as the mothers we now have today.

Imagine the sorrow in our Lady's heart, when she saw what was happening to Christ. Here was a man who had never wanted a single thing for Himself. He had spent His time going around doing good — comforting the sorrowful, healing the sick, raising the dead to life. He was spat upon, stoned, and finally put to death. How easy it would have been for us to have become very angry with God, if we had been in Mary's position! How justified we would have thought ourselves!

Lord, help me to imitate the patience of our Blessed Mother. Help me to realize that what happens to me is not the important consideration. It is my reaction, my conforming myself to Your holy will, that really counts.

. . .the dawn of this world's light.

REV. JOHN R. MAGUIRE

☐ 26 ☐

Our Lady of Vladimir

The F.B.I. files in Washington have 141,231,773 fingerprints which identify 72,089,774 Americans.

Had it been in operation 1900 years ago, it is quite possible that the fingerprints of the Mother of God would be recorded. . . .No such file exists. Yet within our spiritual consciousness we have our own identification bureau. Strange and wonderful things have happened in our lives and we ask ourselves, *"I wonder whose hand is here?"*

If we could check the soul's "fingerprints," we would see that so often the hand is Mary's. . . .She is our tender guide in this voyage through life. Our helper. Our mother.

On that awesome day of judgment, when our Lord and Maker is examining our souls; when all heaven is hushed for the solemn sentence, then Mary's fingerprint — and our love for her — will mean so much.

If we always tried to do what she asked, we can rest assured that His sentence will be light.

Rejoice, glorious Virgin,

PETER V. ROGERS, O.M.I.

☐ 27 ☐

Notre Dame de Monstier — Sisteron, France

The Mother of Jesus had always known the tension of opposites: virginity and motherhood, joy and suffering, the black agony of crucifixion and the white glory of Resurrection. This is reflected in the very names of her Rosary mysteries which recall not only the fact of her divine motherhood, but also the vast divine drama of which she was a part.

Others may ponder the Word of God; she bore the Word Himself in her womb, she made that Word incarnate by her womanhood, nourished His human flesh, and lived with Him for thirty years before anyone heard His words of salvation.

She was the co-laborer of the Holy Spirit in God's greatest human task: the flesh-taking of God Himself, and she received, in a measure equal to her role, the gifts and the outpouring of that Spirit. No other task, not even that of an Apostle, could equal hers.

. . .More lovely than all other virgins

REV. CLIFFORD STEVENS

□ 28 □

Our Lady of Kiova — Poland

"Praise the Lord" is a phrase we hear frequently today. But exactly what do we mean by praising the Lord?

Perhaps we have become accustomed to only talking to the Lord in prayer when we need something. Prayers of praise are not easy for us. Just as we are sometimes shy about giving compliments to others, we are also shy with the Lord in praising and thanking Him for all the wondrous things He has given us.

"God has done great things for me. Holy is his name," proclaimed Mary when visiting her cousin Elizabeth. The Lord also had done mighty things for all of us. We should remember and thank Him each day for the many favors that He has bestowed on us. "My being proclaims the greatness of the Lord and my spirit finds joy in God my savior"— Luke 1.46.

. . .in heaven.

MARGARET HULA MALSAM

□ 29 □

Our Lady of Clermont

After the death of Christ, Mary was made a fulfillment of the Bride of the Canticles, seeking her Beloved with sorrow and the plea: I sought him and found him not. Love and longing were consuming her in the absence of Christ.

Fifteen years of silent waiting in exile from Christ, fifteen years of yearning such as they say mothers only know, and now Mary is on her earthly deathbed. They say that at the hour of death the mind is empowered to cast one great retrospective glance over its life. If that be so, what strange panorama passed before the eyes of Mary. Memories of her Son, yes, but no haunting of sins long buried. For her, therefore, judgment has no terrors, and death can only mean reunion.

When the pure heart of Mary stopped its beating, Jesus came and took His Mother to her everlasting home where He dwells. The Beloved was found by this Bride of the Canticles and His voice was heard: "Arise, make haste, my love, and come."

   . . .*Receive our evening farewell,*

REV. MSGR. JAMES I. TUCEK

□ 30 □

Our Lady of Deliverance — Martinique

The Rosary has been for centuries our most popular prayer and devotion. It is a readily available means for spiritual meditation at any time and place. It has also been the most acceptable and beloved manner of honoring Mary, the Mother of Christ.

Winds of doubt caused by the irresponsible blowing of some who consider themselves experts in matters devotional are bothering a number of the faithful about the efficacy of the Rosary. A few restless souls are dropping their devotional sails to change their course regarding all routine prayer.

These restless persons who deem themselves liberal and progressive believe that the methods for promotion, propaganda, and presentation effectively used by big business should be adopted in matters spiritual. All things routine should be avoided. But note the reliance of big business on routine trademarks, slogans, and catchy phrases — all repeated over and over again via radio, television, newspapers, magazines, billboards.

   . . .*O Mother of beauty,*

MOST REV. ANDREW G. GRUTKA

AUGUST

□ 31 □

Our Lady of Tables — Montpellier

In this short Gospel Jesus gives highest praise to His Mother. Here is the entire passage: The mother and brothers of Jesus came to be with him, but they could not reach him because of the crowd. He was informed, "Your mother and your brothers are standing outside and wish to see you." He told them in reply, "My mother and my brothers are those who hear the word of God and act upon it."

Mary is the perfect exemplar of the receptive hearer. This passage is similar to another in Luke (11.27-28), a Gospel pericope used in many Masses in honor of our Blessed Mother. Jesus again says of her that she is blessed for hearing the Word of God and keeping it. As Luke records in his second chapter, Mary pondered the Word of God in her heart — Luke 2.19.

Dear Mother of the Word Incarnate, teach us to be docile to the Holy Spirit as you were, so that Christ, the Word of God, may be formed in us and we will reflect the glory of Jesus to others.

. . .and for us plead with Christ your Son. Amen.

SISTER ELIZABETH ANN CLIFFORD, O.L.V.M.

SEPTEMBER

□ 1 □

Our Lady of Olives

Ein Karem near Jerusalem is a pretty village, terraced with grapevines and olive trees. Here Zachary and Elizabeth lived for many years in a childless marriage. When Elizabeth conceived John the Baptist, in her old age, she praised God for taking away the shame of her barrenness among men.

Zachary's reaction? He doubted the angel who came to bring him the good news. He was struck dumb until the moment he named his son John. But when Mary came to Ein Karem to tell her good news to her cousin Elizabeth, John leapt in the womb.

How do we receive the message of Christ? Do we doubt the good news and remain mute? Or do we praise God for showing us the way to a fruitful life on earth?

The Memorare: Remember, O most gracious Virgin Mary,

REV. MSGR. JOHN G. NOLAN

☐ 2 ☐

Our Lady of Ebron — Germany

Modern Bible studies have made us aware of the presence of Mary the Mother of Christ, in the scriptures more than ever before. No longer is the no-no attitude prevalent in the Catholic Church about reading the Bible. Other Christians also have been discovering Mary through Scripture.

The Mother of Christ can be the needed intercession between Catholics and other Christians. Words often can be without meaning when hearts and minds seem to wander away from their spiritual purpose. The Mother of Jesus is the element that can mend, heal, and bind common purpose in a loving Christian ideal.

The role of Mary in the Catholic Church and other Christian churches can establish blessings, graces, and Christian love uniting thoughts and actions centered on her beloved Son's Christian message.

. . .*that never was it known*

JOHN JULIUS FISHER

☐ 3 ☐

Our Lady of Good Shepherd

Our perfect pattern! When our Blessed Lord ascended into heaven, and a cloud received Him out of sight, we can imagine what love was poured forth upon His Mother by those who had watched Him go from them into heaven, and who knew what she had been to Him on earth.

Consider what a perfect pattern she must have been to them of one whose heart was "always fixed on heavenly things."

We look up today to see our Lord ascended, Conqueror of death forevermore; and we beseech Mary to teach us how to live our lives like hers above earthly things, with our conversation in the heavens, feeding like her upon the very Body and Blood of Christ, until we too shall be received into heaven, our fatherland, to be forever with the Lord.

. . .*that anyone who fled to your protection,*

ALBERT A. MURRAY, C.S.P.

SEPTEMBER

□ 4 □

Our Lady of Koden, Ziemia Lubelska — Poland

Michelangelo, in sculpturing his famous Pieta, portrayed the Virgin Mother seated, holding the lifeless corpse of her Divine Son in her arms. Her face is sad, yet composed in dignity. Pity is there, too, and strength in abundance. What a nightmare our Lady went through at the crucifixion; yet she didn't crack nor break.

At some time in our own life a terrible shock or blow may come. If tragedies happen to other people, who is to say that we alone will be spared? In time of sorrow or crisis we need strength to carry on, not only for ourselves, but for others who may depend on us.

Remember that in her hour of agony, the Blessed Virgin did not collapse. The Evangelist says, "There stood by the cross of Jesus, Mary His Mother." Be prepared to stand by the cross.

. . .*implored your help, or sought your intercession*

EDWIN R. MC DEVITT, M.M.

□ 5 □

Our Lady of the Woods — France

The appearances of our Lady at Lourdes bring to mind the virtue of humility. The apparitions inspired Bernadette to a faithful imitation of Mary's sanctity. Following Mary's footsteps is living a life hidden in God. It is a sharing in her humility.

What is humility? Humility is a pleasing virtue. The humble person recognizes his need for God and for others. He realizes God's blessings and gifts. Whatever talents he possesses he knows them as gifts of God. Whatever success he attains he knows comes from God and the assistance of others. Honestly, he can say as St. Paul did: "By the grace of God I am what I am." Mary said: "He who is mighty has done great things to me."

Humility is a Christian virtue and goes hand in hand with initiative, energy, creativity. God's gifts are given us for our own good and for the good of others.

. . .*was left unaided.*

MARIE LAYNE

SEPTEMBER

☐ 6 ☐

Our Lady of Guadalupe — Spain

Christ's royalty rests on two fundamental principles: the natural right of His divine personality and the acquired right because of mankind's redemption carried out by Him.

Mary's royalty lies the same way in her Divine Motherhood and in her Co-Redemption. She was born Queen, full of grace, chosen to be Mother of the King of Kings to help Him to establish on earth the Kingdom of God.

It is significant that the only portrait of Mary given by herself to mankind shows her with royal appearance, as St. John describes her in the Apocalypse. This is the painting of our Lady of Guadalupe given to Juan Diego, in Mexico City in 1531.

Inspired by this confidence,

RICARDO COLIN, M.G.

☐ 7 ☐

Our Lady of Zykrowic — Poland

Tomorrow the liturgy of the Church celebrates the birthday of the Blessed Virgin Mary. Since Christ gave her to all of us to be our Mother — "Son, behold thy Mother" — birthday greetings from all her sons and daughters are very much in order.

Our birthday greetings can best be expressed, I think, in the familiar words the angel spoke announcing that she was to be the Mother of God: "Hail, Mary, full of grace, the Lord is with thee. Blessed art thou among women." Today, then, a Rosary would be especially meaningful and our thoughtfulness and love much appreciated by her. The celebration of Mary's birthday will naturally lead the family of God to the Eucharistic Banquet, which her divine Son Himself has prepared and to which He invites all of us. Happy Birthday, Mary!

. . .I fly to you,

JOSEPH F. HOGAN, S.J.

SEPTEMBER

□ 8 □

Nativity of Mary

This feast celebrates the birth of the most important woman in the history of mankind. Though nothing is mentioned in the inspired Word about Mary's birth or her death, we know that her birth brought to the very eyes of mankind the Predestined Woman who was to be the Mother of Jesus, Savior of the World. Joachim and Anne, her parents, are also honored as saints. Elizabeth and Zachary are her cousins. The Heavenly Father looked down today on this babe who was to be the Mother of His only-begotten Eternal Son.

The celebration of this birth must mean for all the beauty of motherhood, a loving sense of the beautiful duty to train and educate one's children. How joyous must have been the task of Blessed Anne to care for and clothe little Miriam, to nourish her, to teach her to walk, and to teach her to pray, for this babe was to be the Mother of all mankind in and with her Son. No one has learned to pray as she learned to pray.

Today, all mankind prays to her as the Mother of God.

. . .O virgin of virgins, my mother.

EDWIN G. KAISER, C.PP.S.

□ 9 □

Our Lady of Puy

As children we enjoyed birthdays. They were special days and we were treated to happy memories with fun and gifts and perhaps a party and special privileges. Even in later years we find most people celebrating the anniversary day of their birth.

From the early ages of the Church the birthday of our Blessed Lady has been celebrated, and rightly so. Happy was the day of her birth, for Mary had been preserved immaculate from the first moment of her conception. She remained free from all sin, and could be then a worthy Mother to her own Son, Jesus Christ. Mary's birth marked the final step in preparing the world for the coming Savior.

If we celebrate our own birthday, how much more should we celebrate and thank God for the birth of Mary.

. . .To you I come,

MOST REV. ALBERT R. ZUROWESTE

SEPTEMBER

☐ 10 ☐

Our Lady of Tru

The perfect example of humility is seen when St. Elizabeth reminded our Lady of her unique and wonderful position: "Blessed art thou among women and blessed is the fruit of thy womb."

Our Lady makes no attempt to deny this extraordinary position, for — and here is humility — she is incapable of ascribing it to herself: "My soul," she says, "magnifies God . . . He that is mighty has done great things to me."

Humility is the joyful acceptance of the truth about ourselves, that all we have is from God. We have nothing that we have not received. True humility is never separated from supreme confidence. For if all comes from God, there should be no limit whatever to our confidence.

. . .before you I stand,

EUGENE BOYLAN, O.C.S.O.

☐ 11 ☐

Our Lady of Hildesheim

Torchlight processions and crowds in the streets usually mean a football victory, a convention, or the visit of a celebrity. It is hard for us today to believe that the decision of a Church Council could cause such excitement among the people. It started with one shouted Greek word at Ephesus in the year 431: *Theotokos*, "Mother of God." The Christian heart rejoiced that the Christian mind was in agreement. The Church had defined that Christ is God, and Mary is His Mother. The people in the streets shouted because Mary's title was already in their hearts.

It is all in the Hail Mary, as it was really all in the Gospels and the Church teaching from the beginning. First we call upon her who is "full of grace" because "the Lord is with thee." Then we respond, as the early Christians did, "Holy Mary, Mother of God, pray for us sinners."

. . .sinful and sorrowful.

MOST REV. PAUL J. HALLINAN

SEPTEMBER

□ 12 □

Holy Name of Mary

Today we are reminded that the name of Mary means "Star of the Sea" and is thus most appropriately applied to the Virgin Mother of Christ. Her virginity is the star which shines before God and man.

Says the Church in the Breviary: "She is therefore that glorious star. . .lifted above this wild and boundless sea (of life) gleaming with merits and enlightening us by her example. Whoever you are, when you find yourself tossed by storms and tempest upon this world's raging waters. . .never turn your eyes away from the brightness of this star. Think of Mary, call upon Mary, invoke Mary so that you may experience in yourself what has been rightly said "And in the name of the Virgin was Mary."

In these beautiful words of the Church, today, let us find the help and comfort we need in times of trial and distress.

O Mother. . .

REV. MSGR. JAMES. P. CONROY

□ 13 □

Maria Zell — Austria

In the year 1889 Pope Leo XIII wrote: "Now, Venerable Brethren, you know the times in which we live. They are scarcely less deplorable for the Christian religion than the days which in times past were most full of misery of the Church. We see faith, the root of all Christian virtues, lessening in many souls; we see charity growing cold, the young generation daily growing in depravity of morals and views, the Church of Jesus Christ attacked on every side by open force or by craft, a relentless war waged against the Sovereign Pontiff, and the very foundations of religion undermined with a boldness which waxes daily in intensity."

The description fits our times. The powers of evil seek to destroy God and religion. Through prayer, especially the Rosary, each one can fight against the evil in the world today. The Rosary is power. Learn to love and pray it daily.

. . .of the Word Incarnate,

MOST REV. JOHN J. CARBERRY

SEPTEMBER

☐ 14 ☐

Our Lady of Fontevrault

Mary, the Mother of Jesus, stood at the foot of the cross in the company of St. John. Shortly after Jesus gave her to St. John as His Mother and ours, Jesus said, "Now it is finished" and He bowed His head and gave up His spirit. Jesus gave us Mary as our Mother, to whom we can pray for help, and whose virtues we can imitate.

Mary knew the pain of suffering, the pangs of separation, the emptiness of loss. She loves us because Jesus gave us to her to be her spiritual children.

. . .do not ignore my petitions,

MAURUS FITZ GERALD, O.F.M.

☐ 15 ☐

Our Lady of Sorrows;
The Amiable Mother of Starkenburg — Missouri

The sorrows of Mary are all bound up with the sufferings of her Son. Man of Sorrows is the Son of the Mother of Sorrows. Many sorrows afflict us in this life, but there must be a certain priority: first must be the sorrow for our sins which should grow deeper day by day. Especially at the reception of the Sacrament of Reconciliation we must seek the deepening sorrow for sin.

The most difficult sorrow to bear is that which afflicts parents because of the evil deeds of their own children which they themselves may in no way have caused. We must feel deep sorrow over all the evils that afflict men, the sickness, the physical weakness, the helplessness of others. Here our sorrows must mingle with both prayer for them and effort to assist them in their trials. We cannot share with Mary her sorrows without also sharing in her many joys: the blessed company of Joseph, the delights of the little Babe she bore for the salvation of mankind, the glory of the Resurrection and her own blessed Assumption.

. . .but in your mercy hear and pray for us. Amen.

EDWIN G. KAISER, C.PP.S.

☐ 16 ☐

Our Lady of Good News

Mary wants us to help her to bring Jesus into the world. In union with her our work receives new value and is more acceptable to God. The Gospels prove this. It was through Mary that St. John was sanctified; and also Elizabeth. It was through Mary that the shepherds and the kings discovered the Messiah. It was through Mary that Simeon held in his arms the Desire of Nations. It was Mary's prayer that produced the first miracle at Cana. It was Mary that introduced Jesus to His *"hour"* and the Passion.

Mary's journey through life was uphill from Bethlehem to Calvary. If my road, like hers, lies uphill, I shall find strength in Jesus, not only in my arms, but in my heart, in Holy Communion.

When you were baptized, Mary received you from the baptismal font as her child, and became your Mother in a truer sense than your natural mother.

"Go out to all the world, and tell the Good News." — Mark 16.15

MOST REV. REMBERT KOWALSKI, O.F.M. (China)

☐ 17 ☐

Our Lady of Everyday

It is well to start each day by making the Morning Offering. As soon as you arise, bless yourself and say: "O Jesus, through the Immaculate Heart of Mary, I offer Thee my prayers, works, and sufferings of this day for all the intentions of Thy Sacred Heart, in union with the Holy Sacrifice of the Mass throughout the world, in reparation for my sins, for the intentions of all our Associates, and in particular for the intention of the Apostleship of Prayer."

By saying this prayer devoutly, you consecrate every thought, word, and deed to almighty God, thus making them meritorious for you. This is the meaning of the famous saying of St. Paul: "Whether you eat or drink, or whatsoever else you do, do all to the glory of God." Your Morning Offering turns all your thoughts, words, and deeds into prayers.

The Angelus: The angel of the Lord declared unto Mary:

REV. JOHN A. O'BRIEN

□ 18 □

Our Lady of Smelcem

There is a grace, and a beauty about the lovely name of Mary. At one time every family of the faith would try to name at least one daughter Mary.

St. Bernard has a most beautiful sermon on the Holy Name of Mary. He writes: "In danger, in difficulty, or in doubt, think of Mary, call upon Mary. Let her not be absent from your lips or from your heart.

"If you follow her you will never go astray. If you pray to her you will never be drawn into despair. If you keep her in mind you will never wander away. If she holds you, you will never fall. If she leads you, you will never be weary. If she helps you, you will reach home safe at last.

"And in this way, you prove to yourself how justly it is said: 'And the Virgin's name was Mary.' "

. . .And she conceived of the Holy Spirit. Hail Mary. . .

MOST REV. JOHN J. CARBERRY

□ 19 □

Our Lady of LaSalette

The speaker was eloquently denouncing all those who were trying to "downgrade Mary." A woman in the audience asked, "How would it be possible for any mere human to take from or add to what Mary was — the Mother of Jesus Christ?"

The controversy over Mary which has arisen during the post-Conciliar period is actually one of varied "images" by which she is viewed by Catholic people. There are some who cannot see her in any other manner but as a "Queen." Others see her as she appeared at Lourdes, Fatima, Guadalupe, Pontmain, LaSalette, and elsewhere.

No matter by how many different titles she is known, Mary was only one person, a Jewish woman who gave birth to Jesus Christ, the Redeemer of mankind. This was certainly the greatest height to which a woman could be called. No other fact can dwarf this one, that Mary brought our Redeemer into the world.

Behold the handmaid of the Lord:

ANNE TANSEY

SEPTEMBER

□ 20 □

Our Lady of Silver Feet

St. John tells us emphatically that "the world and its lusts are passing away, but the one who does the will of the Father lives forever." Mary is a powerful witness to this truth. May we imbibe her trust that we are blessed as we obey God. Every title given to Mary in her litany will be true to her forever.

I think the message in Luke (2:39-40) is most encouraging. The ordinariness of the lives of Joseph, Mary, and Jesus is put forth, and from that ordinariness "the child grew in wisdom, age, and grace." *No doubt* Joseph and Mary grew also in all these areas. Jesus received no baccalaureate degree and never worked for General Motors. No one nominated Him for an "Oscar" or an "Emmy"; but He knew His Father, and He invited and empowered us to walk with Him in the Father's will and, thereby, live forever.

Lord, take my hand lest I get lost forever.

...Be it done unto me according to thy word. Hail Mary...

SISTER THERESA MOLPHY, C.S.J.

□ 21 □

Our Lady of Pucha — Valencia

St. Paschal Baylon was noted both for his affection for the Mother of God and his keen devotion to the Blessed Sacrament.

Actually, what better way to achieve holiness? Devotion to Mary helps us overcome the pull of passion and refines our spiritual sensitivities. Our Lady, on her part, has never been known to forsake a son or daughter in need.

At Emmaus the two disciples pleaded with Christ, "Stay with us, Lord." With them He only tarried the evening. For the believing Catholic, Christ is present always in the Blessed Sacrament to counsel and to love us. In Holy Communion He comes to make us a part of Him and Himself a part of us.

Truly, like St. Paschal Baylon, our lives have fallen on pleasant places if we continue to love the Eucharist and cherish devotion to our Lady.

And the Word was made flesh:

EDWIN R. MC DEVITT, M.M.

SEPTEMBER

☐ 22 ☐

Our Lady of Valvancre

A̶ll the glory and all of the prerogatives that Christian devotion ascribes to the Blessed Virgin Mary are due to the basic theological truth that she is the Mother of God. No one has ever written a successful biography of Mary, alone. Yet every *Life of Christ* must pay her homage.

Another important facet of Marian devotion is the eminence of the Holy Spirit in her life. She conceives by the power of the Holy Spirit and all spiritual writers tell us that she lived her life under His influence. When the Holy Spirit infused the apostolic Church with life, the *Acts of the Apostles* makes a point of it that Mary, the Mother of Jesus, was there.

Mary certainly had the "baptism of the Spirit" with all that that implies.

. . .And dwelt among us. Hail Mary. . .

REV. CHARLES DOLLEN

☐ 23 ☐

Our Lady of Valvancre — Spain

W̶henever Saturday has no feast of greater rank, the Church dedicates it to the Blessed Mother. In this, the week starts out with our Lord on Sunday and ends with His Blessed Mother on Saturday.

So too, our day should begin with the inspiration of our Lord and end with the dedication to the Blessed Virgin. Much like the children who go forth to their daily cares and come home in the evening to their mother. In this way our lives are lived with God for our deeds are inspired and accomplished by Him and presented at the heavenly throne by His Blessed Mother.

Pray for us, O holy Mother of God:

REV. MSGR. JOSEPH B. LUX

□ 24 □

Our Lady of Ransom

The feast of Our Lady of Ransom originated with the Order of Blessed Mary of Ransom, founded in Spain during the thirteenth century. Members of the Order offered themselves as hostages in exchange for Christian prisoners held by the Moors.

In modern times, the Fathers of Our Lady of Mercy (Mercedarians) are cited by Pope John Paul II as ''an ancient and well-deserving Order, which for over seven and one-half centuries has been doing everything in its power for the most afflicted and oppressed members of the Mystical Body of Christ.'' The mission of St. Peter Nolasco, founder of the Order, is prolonged today . . . ''in service to the faith, giving hope, and offering the assistance of Christ's charity to all who find themselves subjected to new forms of captivity''— in prisons, in urban poverty and hunger, among drug addicts, and in areas where the Church is persecuted or reduced to silence.

. . . That we may be made worthy of the promises of Christ.

ROBERT J. LEUVER, C.M.F.

□ 25 □

Our Lady of Passer

The Son of God, coming from heaven, entered this world through Mary, and therefore, she is called the Gate of Heaven. The Church uses this title with great veneration. Mary, who became the gate of the great King also became the exponent of *blessed light.*

Jesus is the *Light of Light* and His Mother is appropriately called the gate of light. Graciously she alone gave the Savior to the world, becoming the blessed gate; and for this reason, all nations have called her blessed.

Holy Mary sends blessed light to us so that we can expiate our own worldly fears and distractions. When we let our eyes and ears send signals to our human hearts to receive these heavenly ways — all our undesirable dilemmas are expelled.

Pour forth, we beseech thee, O Lord,

JOHN JULIUS FISHER

□ 26 □

Our Lady of Victory

The battle of Lepanto in 1571 saved Christian Europe. Unlike a historian, the Church views such an event personally. She had prayed to the Mother of God, through the Rosary, for the result. The feast then is one of thanksgiving in her honor.

The Rosary has qualities that make it universally popular. It is easy to say. The feel of the crucifix and the beads keep our attention. The prayers are the simple basic ones we all know. The meditations are on the Gospel, a daily reminder of the mysteries of that great act of love which leads to eternal life in God's presence.

When our Lady appeared to Bernadette at Lourdes in 1858, they prayed the Rosary together. Bernadette never forgot the way our Lady taught her to say it. Bernadette tells of one apparition. "The Lady's eyes left me for a moment and looked into the distance above my head. When she looked at me again I asked what had made her so sad and she said simply, 'Pray for sinners!' " The world needs the Rosary!

. . .*thy grace into our hearts,*

GEORGE M. BUCKLEY, M.M.

□ 27 □

Our Lady of Happy Assembly

At the Annunciation, Mary first acted as intercessor between God and man and man and God. Through this act of intercession man was given Christ.

Fittingly we pay honor to Mary. But the mother wants not glory or honor for herself, rather she wants it for her Son. His will is her will, and His will is that all men in community bring that community to God the Father. One aspect or method of bringing the community to God is the inward betterment of that community. Through the three children at Fatima in 1917, Mary promised help to those people who would observe regular confession, reception of the Eucharist, prayer, and meditation on the mysteries of the Rosary.

To Jesus through Mary is the Christian's objective. Together with Mary and all the saints and Jesus we may then approach God. Our community, the Church, the saints, Mary and Joseph and Jesus all are a means to the end, God, our eternal Father.

. . .that we, to whom the Incarnation of Christ, thy Son,

ROBERT G. LEE

□ 28 □

Our Lady of Cambron

Papal encyclicals are usually heavy documents to read. However, occasionally a paragraph with a warm human appeal is found. Such is a reference to our Lady which appears in Pope Pius XII's letter to the world for the centenary of her apparition at Lourdes:

"Just as all mothers are deeply affected when they perceive that the countenance of their children reflects a peculiar likeness to their own, so also our most Sweet Mother wishes for nothing more, never rejoices more, than when she sees those whom, under the cross of her Son, she has adopted as children in His stead, portray the lineaments and ornaments of her own soul in thought, word and deed."

This is saying that a mother loves to be told that her child looks like and acts like her. Is not this very natural? Mary, therefore, rejoices when we so think and act that we resemble her.

. . .was made known by the message of an angel,

MOST REV. JOHN J. CARBERRY

□ 29 □

Our Lady of Tongres

The great Cardinal Newman, one of the most brilliant men of modern times, wrote beautifully about God and composed many lovely prayers:

"O my God, let the breathing of my soul be with Jesus, Mary, and Joseph."

"O God, I come to you in great fear but in greater love. O may I never lose my youthful eager love for you, as the years pass away, and the heart shuts up, and all things are a burden. Make your grace, Lord, supply for the failure of my nature. Do you for me, the less I can do for myself. And the more I refuse to open my heart to you, so much the fuller and stronger may your visits be to me."

"O Heart of Jesus, all Love; O holy Heart most lovely, I adore you through all moments while I breathe, even to the end of my life. Amen."

. . .may, by his Passion and Cross, be brought to the glory of his resurrection.

REV. RAWLEY MYERS

□ 30 □

Our Lady of Beaumont

Mary is not a goddess, but a human being, one of us. Our reason for honoring her is that she of all of us was closest to the redeeming work of Christ. Physically, she bore Him within her. Even more importantly she, first among all of us, responded to what He was. She first said "Amen," to the mission of Jesus Christ, and responded with her complete being.

Mary is the first-fruit of the Redemption. In this her honor lies. And besides, we give her our affection and imitation.

Through the same Christ our Lord. Amen.

GILBERT ROXBURGH, O.P.

OCTOBER

□ 1 □

Our Lady of the Holy Rosary — Cracow, Poland

October is dedicated to the Queen of the Holy Rosary. And just what is the Rosary? It is a form of prayer in which beads are passed between the fingers. The Apostles' Creed is said while holding the crucifix; the Our Father is said on the large beads, and the Hail Mary is said on the small beads. After each group of Hail Marys, one says "Glory be to the Father."

While saying the "decades" of Hail Marys, we generally meditate on some mystery from the life of our Lord or His Blessed Mother. The daily entries in this book afford some thoughts for these reflections.

The beads are a tangible means of keeping our minds on God and His Blessed Mother. Just to touch them in our purse or pocket is like putting our hand for a moment in hers. The Rosary has been called a bouquet of fresh, fragrant flowers culled from the human heart.

Regina Caeli — Queen of Heaven. . .

PATRICK PEYTON, C.S.C.

□ 2 □

Our Lady of Tuchow — Poland

We owe the dedication of this month to our Blessed Mother under the title of "Our Lady of the Rosary" to the personal love of Pope Leo XIII (1878-1903). He was devoted to the Rosary and tried to restore it to the flourishing state in which it had been before it lost favor with the people.

We may indeed thank God for our times when the Rosary is known, loved, and recited in every language by millions the world over.

October is with us once more. . .may it mean a rededication to our Blessed Mother under this beautiful title of "Our Lady of the Rosary." It will be most pleasing to her if we are determined to recite the Rosary very humbly, prayerfully, and meditatively as well as joyfully each single day, not only during this month, but every day of our lives.

. . .*O Queen of Heaven, rejoice;*

MOST REV. JOHN J. CARBERRY

□ 3 □

Our Lady of the Place — Rome

The words "My being proclaims the greatness of the Lord" (Luke 1.46) contain Mary's own version of her place in the Church. It is one which no one can dispute or take away. It does not depend upon any apparition or devotion. Mary is the Mother of Jesus Christ. How could she hold any greater honor than that?

The world was shocked in November, 1972, when a vandal damaged the *Pieta*, a work Michelangelo sculptured in 1498 and which has been treasured in St. Peter's Basilica, Rome. It represents Mary holding her dead Son in her arms.

In early spring of 1973 the *Pieta* was back in St. Peter's restored, cleaned, and more beautiful than ever. What some misguided man had destroyed was repaired by others. We are all brothers and sisters in Christ, and Mary holds all of us in her heart.

. . .*alleluia!*

ANNE TANSEY

OCTOBER

□ 4 □

Our Lady of the Cape — Cap de la Madeleine, Canada

A pilgrimage to the Canadian shrines is an experience that can only be lived to be understood. The faith of the crowds can almost be felt, it is so intense and so genuine. The candlelight processions, the songs, and the sense of sharing make it an event to be remembered, and savored with each recall.

Another famous shrine is that of St. Anne de Beaupre in Quebec. Traditions reaching back to the second century name the parents of the Blessed Virgin as Anne and Joachim. We can only surmise that they were typical Jewish figures of their time, devout and regular in their service of the Jewish religion.

St. John Damascene, writing in the eighth century, recounts the tradition that tells us that St. Anne was sterile until a relatively mature age and then she conceived Mary. One thing we can be certain of — the whole world has benefited through their child.

. . .*For he whom thou didst merit to bear —*

REV. CHARLES DOLLEN

□ 5 □

Notre Dame de Buch — Pire Mountains, Guienne, France

God's handmaiden boasts of future fame. Her song—The Magnificat — is a tapestry of praises from the past, typical of the rich literature of Israel. How short-lived were the glories of Annunciation.

How many times the young woman must have felt, like the other saints— Lord, it is no wonder You have so few friends. You take such poor care of them. To see the face of Joseph outraged with dismay and sadness; the incrimination of friend and kin; the journey to Bethlehem and all the privations of that stable; the years of obscurity in which she raised a carpenter's son whom she was told was to be a King — how many things Mary must have kept in her heart!

One of our least inspired inclinations is to conclude that Mary could tolerate all this difficulty with superb ease because, after all, she is the Mother of God and never worried because she knew everything would turn out well. She didn't know. She *believed!*

. . .*alleluia!*

REV. RALPH HARTMAN

OCTOBER

□ 6 □

Our Lady of La Plebe — Venice

Let us take our stand in front of that earthly and divine home of holiness, the House of Nazareth. How much we have to learn from the daily life which was led within its walls! What an all-perfect model of domestic society! Here we behold simplicity and purity of conduct, perfect agreement and unbroken harmony, mutual respect and love — not of the false and fleeting kind, but that which finds both its life and its charm in devotedness of service.

Here is the patient industry which provides what is required for food and raiment; which does so "in the sweat of the brow"; which is contented with little, and seeks rather to diminish the number of its wants than to multiply the sources of its wealth. Better than all, we find here that supreme peace of mind and gladness of soul which never fail to accompany the possession of a tranquil conscience. — Pope Leo XIII, *Papal Documents on Mary.*

. . .*Has risen as he said;*

MOST. REV. LEO A. PURSLEY

□ 7 □

Feast of the Most Holy Rosary

Today's feast recalls the great victory of the Christian navies at Lepanto on Sunday, October 7, 1571, when the forces of Islam were defeated in that historic battle. Today we fight not only against the physical enemies of the Church, but against the great enemy, the devil himself. The liturgy of the Church, today, prays that the Lord "will lead us through His sufferings and death to the glory of His resurrection."

Our Blessed Lady's Rosary recounts the great mysteries of instances in our Lord's life and the role Mary played in them. Each time we say her Rosary, we are not mumbling meaningless words. Rather, we are reliving those great events, those great moments in our Redemption, that have led us "through His suffering and death to the glory of His resurrection." This is the bedrock of our faith.

Lord, each time I pray Your Mother's Rosary, may I renew my faith in Your work of Redemption.

Practice: Always carry a rosary with you. It shows you are Mary's child.

. . .*alleluia!*

REV. THOMAS J. CARPENDER

□ 8 □

Our Lady of Gifts — Avignon

Mary was adorned with sanctifying grace from her conception. "Hail, full of grace" was the angelic salutation, full of all the beauty that enchants God and attracts love.

Did Mary know she was conceived immaculate? Likely not until Gabriel saluted her. Never corrupted by original sin, she experienced no concupiscence within. From without, being human like the rest of mankind, she might have felt the first tiny movements to impatience or envy, but all were quickly suppressed by the preventive grace of God. God loved her — nothing else mattered.

Even had the Blessed Mother known she was immaculate, she would have fled the least occasion of sin lest the beauty of her soul be marred. Confounded by Gabriel's message, she humbly gloried in God's loving choice of her to be His Mother.

V. Rejoice and be glad, O Virgin Mary;

JOSEPH A. VAUGHAN, S.J.

□ 9 □

Our Lady of Ephesus — Moscow

The Dogma of the Divine Maternity of our Lady was defined at the Council of Ephesus, A.D. 431, and "so great was the devotion of the Faithful of Ephesus to Mary as the Mother of God, and intense their love, that on hearing the decision of the Bishops of the Council they acclaimed them with outpouring of joy, and organizing a procession with blazing torches they accompanied them to their homes" — Pope Pius XI, *Lux Veritatis*, Dec. 25, 1931.

OCTOBER

Listen to the words of St. Thomas Aquinas concerning this glory of Mary: "The Blessed Virgin as Mother of God derives from this infinite Being Who is God, a dignity which in a certain sense is infinite; and as there is nothing more excellent than God Himself, so nothing could have been created more excellent than Mary."

Let us rejoice today in the honor which is Mary's and thank God for having given her also to us as our spiritual Mother.

. . .*alleluia!*

MOST REV. JOHN J. CARBERRY

□ 10 □

Madonna of the Cloister — Besancon

Somehow her months — May and October — and her day, Saturday, are apt, in the way that an artist knows that some work or part of it belongs as it is. May speaks of Mary's purity, joy and femininity. October is the month wherein we understand the fullness of her womanhood. The autumn colors have changed from pastels to flaming brilliance and deep richness, as did her life in which she said "yes" to all that God asked of her.

In the same way, Saturday is appropriate for her, for Saturday was once the traditional day to clean the house, for baths, for Catholics to go to confession — the day to get ready for Sunday.

You have a difficult confession to make? Ask Mary to go with you. Your life needs order in its confusion, cleaning out of old bitterness, a sense of warmth where there is coldness? Ask Mary, who made a home for Jesus, to make of your heart, a home for Him, too.

R. For the Lord has risen indeed;

TERRY MARTIN

□ 11 □

Maternity of the Blessed Virgin Mary

On the feast of the Maternity of the Blessed Virgin Mary we would do well to consider our dispositions because no one comprehends them better than mothers. Fortunately our spiritual dispositions are capable of renovation no matter the state of deterioration that may plague them. The confessional is a perfect repair shop. Just-like-new results are guaranteed if sincerely desired. Miraculous transformations are possible with proper contrition.

If the spiritual state of our souls is in order we can approach our heavenly Mother with any problem, fully confident of a favorable reception. In the *Memorare* we pray: "Never was it known that anyone who fled to your protection or implored your help was left unaided."

In the final analysis all that we seek is happiness — happiness in time and happiness in eternity. Earthly mothers want their children happy. Our heavenly Mother wants us to be happy always.

. . .*alleluia!*

MOST REV. ANDREW G. GRUTKA

□ 12 □

Our Lady of the Pillar — Saragossa, Spain

Jesus' words, "Woman, behold your son. . . . Behold your mother," mean more than just commending her to the care of John.

Marian scholar Eamon Carroll, O. Carm., writes: "The word, 'woman,' finds an explanation in the Savior's farewell discourse at the Last Supper. To strengthen His followers, Jesus recalled an example from the Bible: 'A woman about to give birth has sorrow because her hour has come. But when she has brought forth the child, she no longer remembers the anguish for her joy that a man is born into the world.' Israel's longing for the messianic age was sometimes compared to labor pains. The daughter of Zion has been promised a progeny that would include all races, all nations. The words of Jesus announce the fulfillment of that promise, for Mary on Calvary symbolized the 'woman' who is mother Church, new Israel, new People of God, mother of all, Jew and Gentile."

. . .*O God, who gavest joy to the world.*

FELICIAN A. FOY, O.F.M.

□ 13 □

Our Lady of Fatima — Final Apparition in 1917;
Notre Dame de Clairvaux — France

At Fatima, our Blessed Lady revealed herself as Queen of the Rosary and asked urgently for its recitation as a most powerful means of sanctification and intercession. We may be quite sure, then, that the Rosary is a devotion most pleasing to God and sanctifying for ourselves.

The Rosary is unique in that it is a combination of mental and vocal prayer; in fact, the former is the more important part of it. The beads we pass through our fingers, the Hail Marys and Our Fathers are really no more than an accompaniment of our meditation of the mysteries. These fifteen mysteries, joyful, sorrowful, and glorious, are admirably chosen to give us an insight into the fullness of our faith. For in the Incarnation, the Passion, and the Resurrection are contained the principal mysteries of our religion; and in meditation on these mysteries we re-enact, so to speak, the seasons of the liturgical year.

. . .through the resurrection of thy Son,

G. JOSEPH GUSTAFSON, S.S.

□ 14 □

Our Lady of Larochette — near Geneva, Switzerland

It was not by some divine whim, or as an afterthought, that God caused our Lady to be assumed into heaven "when the course of her earthly career was completed." Mary now shares body and soul in the bliss of everlasting life because she was spotless in body and soul throughout her years here on earth. So, in the feast we celebrate today, we are given a preview of the generosity with which God will reward all those who do His will.

The humiliation of the grave is part of the price we must pay for our wickedness. Soiled with so many past sins, we know that our bodies must be returned to dust. But if we are not fit to enter into the full enjoyment of heaven when our days here are past, we can look up to Mary and glimpse the joy which we too will share when at length God fashions a new heaven and a new earth.

. . .our Lord Jesus Christ:

REV. FRANCIS R. MOESLEIN

☐ 15 ☐

At the Temple — in a confirmation of His presentation — we find the young man Jesus speaking to the Temple leaders. He is demonstrating to His elders what they want to see and hear: a boy deeply concerned about His faith, a boy who is unashamed to speak what He has studied.

There is a genuine sharing here as the leaders realize that they too can learn — even from one so young. There is a common searching for what is important and valuable. Perhaps young and old today have lost that spirit of searching, that love of learning together. For it is this type of learning that liberates our minds and opens our spirits. We think and read about contemporary issues and issues of faith, not for what it can bring us materially, but simply for the insight it gives us into those deepest aspects of our lives.

. . .grant that we may obtain,

JAMES MICHAEL SULLIVAN

☐ 16 ☐

Our Lady of Purity — Celebrated in Many Places

Mary was the most pure creature that ever walked on the face of mother earth. But, unfortunately, so many of us have lost the real meaning of what that means. Her purity was not confined to the realm of sexual morality. It embraced a total way of living.

To be pure of heart means to have a singleness of intention. Purity of heart means that we have given our heart to God with no strings attached. Such purity moves us to act with the single motive of doing everything for the love of God. Such purity makes us the most happy and carefree creatures in the world. In giving ourselves totally to God, we discover that God in turn is able to fill us totally with Himself. In having nothing of self, we wake up having everything of God.

We pray that Mary will help us to become pure of heart.

. . .through his Virgin Mother, Mary,

REV. VINCENT A. YZERMANS

☐ 17 ☐

Notre Dame de Chartres — France
Grotto Dedicated in A.D.40

The Rosary is Mary's pride and joy. Often, she pleaded that more people pray the Rosary. Theologians tell us the ideal form of saying the Rosary is to offer the prayer to the Eternal Father "in honor of the Immaculate Heart of Mary."

Mary can save souls only through the power of God. Being permitted to bring souls to Him, she is happy by renewed and intense devotion to the Precious Blood of her Divine Son. During her life on earth, Mary grieved many times for the injustice and sufferings to which her Son was subjected.

We must love Mary, Queen of Heaven and Earth, and the best way to show our love for the Mother of God, and our Heavenly Mother, is by showing love and devotion to her Son. There is a very close bond between the Precious Blood of Christ and the Immaculate Heart of Mary. Let us always keep this thought in mind when we pray the Rosary.

. . .the joys of everlasting life.

MARIE LAYNE

☐ 18 ☐

Our Lady of Rheims — A.D.405

The month of October has also been designated to the giving of some special honor to St. Joseph through a beautiful prayer to be recited after the Rosary. It is a prayer which confidently implores the protection of St. Joseph in our daily needs.

When it comes to the matter of providing protection, St. Joseph has no peer. Almighty God, in His infinite wisdom, chose St. Joseph to be the earthly protector of the Divine Son and His Blessed Mother. No one else has ever had or could ever have a more important protective assignment! And, there was no earthly peril or difficulty from which St. Joseph did not protect them.

The Litany of St. Joseph rightly refers to him as the "guardian of virgins," "pillar of families," "solace of the afflicted," "hope of the sick," "most strong," and " most faithful." Daily, St. Joseph proves to those who honor him his worthiness to these appellations!

...Through the same Christ our Lord. Amen.

REV. MSGR. RALPH G. KUTZ

□ 19 □

The Inner Life of Mary — Sulpicians

St. Joachim and St. Anne were of the royal house of David. Their lives were wholly occupied in prayer and good works. One thing only was wanting in their union. They were childless, and this was held as a bitter misfortune among the Jews. At length, when Anne was an aged woman, Mary was born, the fruit rather of grace than of nature, and the child more of God than of man. With the birth of Mary the aged Anne began a new life. She watched Mary's every movement with revered tenderness and felt herself sanctified by the presence of her immaculate child.

When Mary was three years old, Anne and Joachim led her up the Temple steps and saw her pass by herself into the inner sanctuary. . . . It was St. Epiphanius who wrote: "Furthermore, these three, Joachim and Anne and Mary, offered a sacrifice of praise to the Trinity."

Learn from them to reverence a divine vocation as the highest privilege, and to sacrifice every natural tie at the call of God.

A Marian Prayer: You are fair, O Mary:

JANE J. STEFANCIC

□ 20 □

Immaculate Heart of Mary — Marianist Missal

Devotion to the Immaculate Heart of Mary began in the early days of the Church. St. Jerome said, "As many wounds as were inflicted on the body of Jesus, were torn in the heart of Mary." From St. Augustine, we learn, "Maternal affinity would have profited Mary nothing had she not first conceived Jesus in her heart."

St. John Vianney provided us with a superb image for reflection and great consolation when he wrote. "The heart of Mary is so tender toward us that hearts of all others in the world put together could not be compared to hers."

Our meditation can center on how much Mary must have pleased God by her perfect conformance with His will; and what her example in this direction can do for us when we are asked to submit to God's will in our lives. Mary's quiet heroism is a precious legacy for people of all times in all places and circumstances.

. . . *The original stain is not in you.*

ANNE TANSEY

□ 21 □

Our Lady of Talan — Dijon, France

The heart of the Mother of God is the heart of the Mother of Mankind. For this reason it is always inclined to us, ready to obtain for us from God the graces we need.

The greatest gift of all, however, which we can obtain from the loving heart of Mary, is that we be inflamed by the same divine fire which consumed her — the fire of divine love. Love of God and love of neighbor: in these two is contained the entire substance of God's law. Living in charity, we imitate the Mother of God and conform ourselves to the wishes of our Redeemer, we live "according to His heart."

With confidence we go to the throne of grace, so that we may obtain mercy and find grace in seasonable aid.

. . . *You are the glory of Jerusalem,*

SEBASTIAN V. RAMGE, O.C.D.

□ 22 □

Notre Dame de Boulogne-sur-Mer — France;
Our Lady of Kazan — Village along Volga River in Russia

Perhaps no prayer to our Lady is more widely loved and used than the *Salve Regina*. What a fitting hymn to praise our Mother, especially during this month.

She is our Holy Queen because of the impeccable beauty of her life which gave human flesh to the King of Kings. Being the Mother of the Savior, she is also the Mother of Mercy. If Jesus could speak of the prodigal son, the wandering sheep, and the lost pieces of silver, are we not right in saying that His pity and concern for men was partly a human gift from a compassionate Mother?

If our sins discourage us, if the past rises up to haunt us, if we have no human friend to go to, turn to our Mother of Mercy. Her Son always took a hint from her.

. . . *You are the joy of Israel,*

EDWIN R. MC DEVITT, M.M.

□ 23 □

Our Lady of Comfort — Honfleur, France

At times, our world seems to be a vale of tears. Many sorrows often burden our normal way of life. There is one who will comfort us during these troubled and trying times. That one person is our Divine Mother.

Mary, our Spiritual Mother, is appropriately called Comforter of the Afflicted. Mary extends hope, and she can change our bitterness and remove the element of sorrow from our troubled lives. If we invoke her patiently and sincerely, she will console us. Mary always has a listening ear.

Sin and temptation can be removed from our minds and hearts, if we let Mary comfort us and let her set in motion new ideals to remove afflictions prying at our physical nature.

. . . *You are the great honor of our people,*

JOHN JULIUS FISHER

□ 24 □

Our Lady of Hermits — Switzerland

Three passages in the second chapter of the Gospel according to Luke portray Mary as a woman of faith who witnessed, remembered, and wondered about the meaning of early events in the life of Jesus.

The events were the visit of shepherds to the manger where He was born; the prophetic meeting and statement of Simeon after the presentation and purification in the Temple, and the finding of Jesus in Jerusalem where He had absented Himself from her and Joseph to be in His

Father's house. Mary kept all these things in memory, and reflected and marveled about them.

Mary was a contemplative person whose reflection led gradually, through the action of the Holy Spirit, to full understanding of the mystery of Jesus' person and mission. Similar contemplation and wonder can lead to understanding and appreciation of the presence and action of God in our lives.

... *You are the advocate of sinners.*

FELICIAN A. FOY, O.F.M.

□ 25 □

Our Lady of Toledo — Spain

When Bourges, Spain, was finally held by the Christian forces during the civil war in the 1930s, a Mass of thanksgiving was offered. The archbishop took a crown of precious jewels from the statue of the Blessed Mother and gave it to the victorious general as a token of appreciation. Accepting the crown, the general said: "I will replace this crown with a crown more precious." He then had the bullets removed from the bodies of the men who died in the battle. From these he fashioned a crown. To this day it adorns the statue of the Blessed Mother in the cathedral, there.

Devotees of Mary can relate to this. Here is our queen wearing a crown fashioned from the sweat, tears, and life's blood of her followers.

This is the kind of devotion that Mary inspires and merits. We too can fashion a crown for her from the substance of our daily living.

... *O Mary, O Mary,*

ALBERT J. NIMETH, O.F.M.

□ 26 □

Our Lady of Victory

On October 7, 1571, Don John of Austria led a Christian flotilla against the Turks and defeated them at Lepanto. Europe was thus saved from possible destruction. To commemorate the victory, Pope (St.) Pius V established the date as the feast of the Rosary. Leo XIII gave the feast additional rank and added the office. We know how richly indulgenced is the Rosary itself.

"Mary's Psalter," it has been called, the full one hundred fifty Aves are considered as a popular substitute for the psalms of the office. But the Rosary is never meant to be a substitute for the liturgy. It is a private devotion that should never interfere with our active participation in liturgical worship.

It should, however, be recited daily. The mysteries focus on key scenes in the drama of our redemption. We start with the Annunciation and finish with Mary's Coronation in heaven — a suggestion of our own ultimate victory.

. . .*Virgin most prudent,*

REV. FRANCIS X. CANFIELD

□ 27 □

Our Lady of the Basilica

Built around 350, during the pontificate of St. Liberius, the massive edifice is also called Basilica Liberiana. The original name was Santa Maria ad Nives, or, "Our Lady of the Snows." Legend relates a wealthy holy Roman was told, in a dream, to honor our Lady with a church. In midsummer, he found part of the Esquiline Hill covered with snow, outlining shape and size of the Basilica. Since Pope Liberius erected the Basilica, the greatest treasure has been an image of the Madonna with the Child Jesus.

St. Helena, mother of Constantine the Great, brought the image to Rome. She visited the Holy Land, during the third century, in an effort to save the remnants of the Holy Places. The people of Rome went to the image to invoke the intercession of our Lady whenever danger prevailed.

It also is known as "Santa Maria Al Prescepe" (St. Mary of the Crib), because tradition relates it has a manger from the stable at Bethlehem. Here, people come to her from all over the world to find peace and refuge.

. . .*Mother most merciful,*

MARIE LAYNE

□ 28 □

Our Lady of the Trellis — Lille, France

When the Angel Gabriel announced to Mary that she was to be the Mother of God, he hailed her as "full of grace." Well may we take that cue and apply it throughout our lives, not only in a spiritual sense, but in a physical sense and in our attitude, as well.

The art of growing old gracefully has always been admired and imitated; observing it can be a privilege and a joy. Those who fight the aging process are to be pitied. Accepting criticism gracefully has a charm to be envied and the wise person doing so grows both in wisdom and stature. Accepting compliments gracefully is no less a charm, either. It is a challenge to be praised and still handle nice words with dignity and real humility.

Gracefulness can be born of spiritual grace. . .intangible loveliness which springs from within and is inspired through prayer and love of Christ.

. . .pray for us.

JO CURTIS DUGAN

□ 29 □

Our Lady of Orope — near Bielle, Savoy, France

St. Luke tells us much of what we know of the Blessed Virgin and one precious detail is that she kept in her memory these mysterious events which came to the Evangelist's knowledge when he set out to write his account of the events "exactly as they were handed down by eyewitnesses" (Luke 1.2).

We should learn from our Blessed Mother to store up and treasure the record of God's dealings with us, keeping at least a mental diary of the great moments in our lives when God has been closest to us, spoken to us, touched our lives. This record will not only contain moments of joy, for God also visits us in times of sorrow. He makes us enter more deeply within ourselves in prayer when we face death or some other tragedy and we ask what He would have us learn, as Mary did in her hidden life at Nazareth.

. . .Intercede for us with our Lord Jesus Christ. Amen.

VINCENT P. MALLON, M.M.

OCTOBER

□ 30 □

Notre Dame de Mondevi — Vie, in Piedmont, France

We began the month of October with our Lady's Rosary; it will be well indeed to have that be our farewell thought for the month.

Through the Rosary we offer to Mary the tribute of our hands, as we fondly slip the beads through the fingers. The very holding of the Rosary in the hands is a source of strength — try it. Further, we offer to our loving Mother through her beads the tribute of our speech as we recite the precious prayers which compose the Rosary.

Especially through the Rosary we offer the tribute of our mind by meditating upon the mysteries of her Rosary, so filled with meaning; and to her we offer the tribute of our will by determination to imitate and practice the virtues which shine forth in her life and her Rosary.

"I would conquer the world if I had an army which recites the Rosary"— Pope Pius IX.

MOST REV. JOHN J. CARBERRY

□ 31 □

*Consecration of the World to the Immaculate
Heart of Mary — by Pope Pius XII in 1942*

Devotion to our Lady's Heart is analogous to that of the Sacred Heart of Jesus, and consists in veneration of her heart of flesh, united to her person, as representing her love, especially her love for her Divine Son, her virtues, and her inner life.

Traces of this devotion can be found in some early commentaries on the Song of Songs, but it was first considerably fostered by St. John Eudes in the seventeenth century. It was Pope Pius VII who gave permission for a feast of the Pure Heart of Mary in 1805.

In more recent times words attributed to our Lady at Fatima have had very strong influence in popularizing the devotion, and on October 31, 1942, Pope Pius XII consecrated the whole world to her Immaculate Heart. Shortly afterward, on May 4, 1944, he directed that the corresponding feast should be observed throughout the Western Church on the octave day of the Assumption.

Lord, may all who devoutly celebrate the feast of Mary's Immaculate Heart be blessed according to the wishes of your own Heart.

G. JOSEPH GUSTAFSON, S.S.

NOVEMBER

□ 1 □

Feast of All Saints in Honor of Our Lady

Holiness is usually compared by the foundation, growth, and measure of an accepted saint. Mary earned the title Queen of All Saints because of her complete love for God. God always was and is the source and inspiration of all of Mary's love.

Jesus is the *Holy One* whose love is perfectly reflected in the love exhibited by His Holy Mother. Mary's perfect love is released to all people who have misery and sin; no sinner is forgotten or hated by her.

Mary, Queen of All Saints, joins with her select to embrace the whole of mankind — all creeds, nations, and races of all generations. The breadth and length of her spiritual love is impossible to measure.

The Magnificat: My soul magnifies the Lord, . . .

JOHN JULIUS FISHER

□ 2 □

Our Lady of Emminont

And I always thought heaven was a place of rest! But didn't the young St. Therese say, in effect, that her heaven would be spent working for us?

Well then, it may be taken for granted that the same kind of thing goes for the Holy Mother, since we are all her lucky children, including the Poor Souls.

Today is one of the feasts of our Most Holy Mother. Now who loves her own children more than a good mother? Who can be more solicitous about her Poor Soul children than Mary herself?

And if the maternal love of this Mother could be augmented, it surely would be if she saw her children love one another. So, if we prayerfully and sacrificingly remember that the Poor Souls are our brothers and sisters, all children of Mary, we can be certain of an extra special motherly embrace.

. . .and my spirit rejoices in God my Savior,

REV. WILLIAM BOAT

□ 3 □

Our Lady of Rennes

Mary had the comforting presence of St. Joseph when she heard the prophecy of Simeon that a sword would pierce her soul. St. Joseph was also with her during the flight into Egypt, and the search for the twelve-year-old Jesus in Jerusalem.

But when her greatest sorrows came, she had to bear them alone: the meeting on the way to Calvary; standing beneath the cross; the removal of her Son's body from the cross, and the entombment. These sorrows were the price Mary paid for mothering the Redeemer of the human race.

The graces and merits won by Jesus and His Mother continually come to us through her hands. By her compassion for the sufferings of Jesus, she became the Queen of Martyrs. In her own exquisite and indescribable agony she became the Mother of Christ's Mystical Body.

. . .for he has regarded the low estate of His handmaiden.

ALBERT J. NEVINS, M.M.

NOVEMBER

☐ 4 ☐

Our Lady of Port Youis — Milan, Italy

Mary was so very much like the rest of us in so many ways. Her parents were responsible for her coming into the world, just like yours and mine. Her life, both before and after her marriage to St. Joseph, was exactly like the one that thousands of women living today are leading — from all outward appearances.

I must remind myself frequently, Lord, that You want me to be a saint! The task is not an easy one but the opportunity is there. You have given me the very same opportunities to love You, as You gave to Your Mother. Help me to remember to use her life as my model. Each day, in my very ordinary existence, You send me crosses to offer up and joys to thank You for. Help me to recognize them as Mary did.

. . .For behold, henceforth all generations will call me blessed;

REV. JOHN R. MAGUIRE

☐ 5 ☐

Establishment of the First Sodality in the Jesuit College at Rome

Genuine devotion to Mary will lead to an imitation of the virtues that were outstanding in the life of Mary. Humility, faith, obedience to God's will, purity: all stand out. These virtues are sorely needed in the world today and will become present only if the followers of Mary live them.

Genuine devotion inspires us to make the mission that Mary fulfilled our own mission. Mary gave God a human body to function among us. Our task is to allow Christ to come alive once again by allowing Him to use our human faculties to further the fruits of redemption.

To achieve this we need discipline and self-control. In this way we too fashion a crown for our Queen, each act a sparkling diadem. When the bombs of temptation are hurled against us, they will fall at our feet harmless because at our side is Mary with her might and her power against the forces of evil.

. . .for he who is mighty has done great things for me,

ALBERT J. NIMETH, O.F.M.

□ 6 □

Our Lady of Fourviere

Mary's readiness to consent to the will of God is the key to her whole life. It made her available to God as His agent and cooperator in the redemption of men. It made her the Mother of His Son, and the spiritual Mother of us all. God willed to need Mary. He wills also to need us.

The Son could have only one Mother. But he needs many bearers of himself — Christophers — to make himself present and active in the flesh everywhere in our time and in all times.

Mary's answer to her annunciation was yes, without reserve: "Let it be done unto me according to your word." Everything that happened to and through her after that occurred as a consequence of her self-surrender to the will of God. Our response to annunciations of God's will for us should be like hers — ready and without strings attached. If it is, the Son can come again in and through us.

. . .and holy is his name.

FELICIAN A. FOY O.F.M.

□ 7 □

Our Lady of Suffrage

For Mary, the descent of the Holy Spirit upon those gathered in the Upper Room represented the second time that the Spirit of God had come upon her. As we think of this in the third Glorious Mystery of the Rosary, can we doubt that Mary was truly a vessel of election?

In these days of women's liberation, so often carried to grotesque extremes, the example of the Virgin Mother is a beacon of light in a tossed and worried sea. Mary conceived and bore the God-child.

She educated Him, encouraged Him in His ministry, stood by His Cross, believed in His Resurrection and now, filled with the Holy Spirit, she rallies the new Church to missionary endeavors.

What a career! What an exciting life! Holy Virgin of Virgins, be an example to women everywhere!

. . . And his mercy is on those who fear him

EDWIN R. MC DEVITT, M.M.

NOVEMBER

□ 8 □

Our Lady of Hope

From the moment of His conception in Mary's womb, Jesus enjoyed the serene bliss of the Beatific Vision. Although He would live a very down-to-earth life, His earth was a heaven because He always saw His father face-to-face. That is why the soul of Christ did not have the virtue of hope.

Hope is only the earth-covered root of heavenly possession, and Jesus possessed His Father from the first. *Mary's* hope, then, is the most perfect ever bestowed on a human soul.

The Church calls Mary the Mother of Sacred Hope. She is the most exalted model of perfect confidence in God. Hail, Holy Queen, our life, our sweetness, and our hope! After this, our exile, show unto us the blessed fruit of thy womb, Jesus.

. . .from generation to generation.

PATRICK PEYTON, C.S.C.

□ 9 □

Our Lady of Almudena — Madrid, Spain

The month of November offers an opportunity for a prayerful examination of our love and our devotion to Mary.

What is necessary if we are to have a solid devotion to Mary? Is profound theological knowledge required? Not exactly, as there are learned scholars of Mary who are not "children of Mary." On the other hand there is many a humble and even unlettered soul who possesses the secret of Mary's love.

What then is necessary? A humble and sincere yearning to know Mary as a Mother seems a basic need. Love of Mary must be desired on our part and the object of our prayer. Other helps are: to be aware of Mary, to read and study about her, to imitate her, to depend upon her, to speak about her, and to consecrate ourselves to her.

We will know when we have found Mary! She will never let us go.

. . .He has shown strength with his arm,

MOST REV. JOHN J. CARBERRY

☐ 10 ☐

Our Lady of Loreto;
Our Lady of Hope

Mary, our Mother, and the virgin Mother of Christ, can be for us a great sign of hope. She is the only human being, besides her Son, who has been taken into heaven body and soul. As we live our lives on earth, working toward our salvation, she is a model and an inspiration for the human race, that God is faithful to His promise. He will save His people and give everlasting life to those who are faithful to Him.

Mary is also a symbol of hope, when we are downcast and weary in God's service. How many times must she have been weary too, she who lived in complete service to God? And she found her joy and comfort in Him. Surely as we struggle, a short prayer to her, to intercede with her Son, will not go unanswered. We can trust that she will continue to help her children.

. . .He has scattered the proud in the imagination of their hearts,

JAMES M. NUSBAUM, S.J.

☐ 11 ☐

Our Lady's Apparition to Portuguese — 1546

The aim of every artist is to express some idea, some concept, of his mind in the external world. The creative work of God might be viewed in a similar manner. Each one of us is intended to express, in a created way, some idea in God's mind; but since a part is left to our own free will in the work, the result is imperfect. But when our Lady came and was presented in the Temple, the Divine Artist saw His plan perfectly fulfilled. In all truth our Lady could say: "I am the Immaculate Conception" — perfectly corresponding to the desire of God in my regard.

The Angel Gabriel put it perfectly in saying: "Hail! full of grace." No human being was ever so pleasing to God as Mary. She was, and is, God's Masterpiece, among all created persons. It is true her Son would outshine her, but He is a divine person. As a mere creature, Mary was lower than the lowest of the angels. But the grace of God elevated her to her present position of Queen of the Angels and the Saints.

. . .He has put down the mighty from their thrones,

EUGENE BOYLAN, O.C.S.O.

□ 12 □

Our Lady of the Tower — Eriburg, Germany

Jesus'consecration to God in the Temple shatters the modern idea that a liberty which consists in not belonging to anybody or anything frees us to serve others. It is just the other way around. Those who are most consecrated to God and to their task in the world are freest to serve others. For a dedication to our mission demands renunciations which free us from the egoism which holds us back from helping others. By dispossession of himself, man finds himself. By clinging desperately to himself, he loses everything.

When Mary and Joseph took Jesus to the Temple they knew that they were leading Him to liberty. They realized that they were confirming the consecration that He Himself would make. Jesus' consecration to His mission has been our salvation, and our dedication can cooperate in that of others.

. . .and exalted those of low degree;

ROMAN GINN, O.C.S.O.

□ 13 □

Dedication of the Abbey of Bec in Honor of Our Lady

"Besides her place in the liturgy, our Lady has been honored by an amazingly rich variety of extra-liturgical devotional forms. Some of these have a long history. In particular, the Dominican Rosary of fifteen decades links our Lady to her Son's salvific career, from the Annunciation and the joyful events of the infancy and childhood of Jesus, through the sorrowful mysteries of His suffering and death, to His Resurrection and Ascension, and the sending of the Spirit to the Apostles at Pentecost, and concluding with the Mother's reunion with her Son in the mysteries of the Assumption and Coronation.

"It is unwise to reject the Rosary without a trial simply because of the accusations that it comes from the past, that it is repetitious and ill-suited to sophisticated moderns. The scriptural riches of the Rosary are of permanent value" — *The American Bishops' Pastoral Letter on the Blessed Virgin Mary (November, 1973).*

The prayer of today's Mass asks: "May we who meditate on these mysteries of the most holy Rosary of the Blessed Virgin Mary imitate the virtues they proclaim and obtain the rewards they promise."

. . .He has filled the hungry with good things,

THOMAS M. BREW, S.J.

□ 14 □

Madonna of the Grotto — Lamego, Spain

The word "Lourdes" has become synonymous with miraculous cures as a result of the countless physical and spiritual healings which have occurred in this town in France. There, our Blessed Mother appeared on eighteen separate occasions to the young girl Bernadette and requested — among other things — that a chapel be erected at that site.

Our Blessed Mother possesses tremendous powers. As the Mother of our Divine Savior, she is able to obtain from Him favors of all descriptions. This she has done countless times at Lourdes. But not only at Lourdes. She has obtained similar favors at the other famous shrines erected in her honor in other parts of the world. And she obtains favors every day for many persons scattered throughout the world.

Our Blessed Mother loves all of us — her children. She is interested in our spiritual, physical and material welfare. We can be sure that our requests to her will be granted provided that they are in keeping with God's will for us.

. . .and the rich he has sent empty away.

REV. MSGR. RALPH G. KUTZ

□ 15 □

Our Lady of Pignerol — Savoy, France

What's in a name? The University of Notre Dame is named after our Lady. Long before the school became famous as a university, or even as a football team with a national reputation, a certain wealthy Catholic gentleman offered the school a huge sum of money provided that the authorities would change the name of the school to his name. The responsible people turned down this attractive offer. They kept our Lady's name and her banner. Our Lady has repaid that delicate gesture a thousand times.

NOVEMBER

If persons are so devoted to Mary and her name, it is because she represents everything that God expects from the human race. She is our most eloquent reason for success in the eyes of God and the most imitable person for all to follow. What Mary did in responding to the will of God is not what is expected of us, but the way she corresponded to the will of God represents the perfect human behavior. Under her leadership we cannot go wrong.

. . .He has helped his servant Israel,

LOUIS J. PUTZ, C.S.C.

□ 16 □

Our Lady, Health of the Sick — Camillians;
Mother of Divine Providence

"If you remove from your midst oppression, false accusation and malicious speech. . .(God) will renew your strength. . .and you will delight in the Lord." Again through Isaiah comes the call to change, to abandon old ways and follow the Lord. With it comes a promise of healing and happiness, but not necessarily happiness now. The call of Levi in the Gospel suggests that with the call of the Lord comes pain and suffering, suspicion and ridicule, abuse and criticism.

In 1858, God began to teach that lesson anew, through Our Lady of Lourdes to St. Bernadette and through her to us. To and through Bernadette came the call to draw near and follow the Lord. The miraculous waters and physical cures were promises of spiritual healing for those who answer God's call. Yet, in the suffering and derision of Bernadette is the reminder that accepting the call first entails pain, criticism, and rejection.

Jesus, I need Your healing in my own life. Help me answer Your call and seek my happiness in You.

. . .in remembrance of his mercy,

NORMAN PERRY, O.F.M.

□ 17 □

Founding of the Confraternity of Our Lady of Sion in 1393

Mary must have been startled by the message of the angel. Mary never doubted God's promise for a moment. Her faith in the word of God was so great that she believed the almost impossible news of her motherhood.

The faith of Mary should be *our* faith. God is still speaking to every one of us. How do *we* respond? Do we hesitate, or politely listen to God's word and then walk away without saying "yes" to Him? Mary had faith in God's word, and that faith had such wondrous results: Christ was born, and showed us the way to His Father. We are asked to have the same faith in God's word as Mary did, and just as God waited to hear Mary's answer, He now waits to hear our answer. What will it be?

. . .as he spoke to our fathers, to Abraham and to his posterity for ever. — Luke 1.46-55

ROBERT M. CHABAK

□ 18 □

Our Lady of Chiquinquira — near Medellin, Colombia

The love of Mary is an essential part of our Catholic spirituality, it gives our spiritual life a richness. Catholics are sometimes asked by those who are not Catholics why Catholics honor Mary so much.

God has already honored her beyond any honor we could pay her when He chose her out of all generations to be the Mother of His only-begotten Son. If God honored her so greatly, how could we fail to honor her?

She was the Mother of our Lord, she gave Him birth, nurtured Him at her breast, reared Him to manhood and stood beside the cross that day He died. How could we fail to love her? And when we come to her, to ask her intercession, she now, as at Cana, turns us closer to Him.

An Evening Prayer: Alma Redemptoris Mater. . .

DALE FRANCIS

□ 19 □

Our Lady of Good News

As we approach the liturgical season of Advent, we find our Lady praying. She is open to God's Spirit. God gave her a mission, the greatest assignment, indeed, ever given to any human being.

NOVEMBER

Angel Gabriel said: "Hail, full of grace, the Lord is with thee." Up to that time, Mary had no indication of God's mission for her, she simply kept herself open to His will and to His intentions. She prepared herself for whatever His wishes would be. God's plans were far beyond her wildest expectation.

"Ancient of Days asked one lowly and wise to welcome the Bountiful One into her bosom; bestowed blessings, begged to be her Babe." Thus does an ancient poem read. God *asked* her, He came to her, He waited on her word.

There is a powerful lesson here. God, sometimes, does wait on our word. God, sometimes, does look for something from us. We must hold ourselves in readiness for whatever His intentions may be.

. . .*Gentle Mother of our Redeemer,*

BLASE SCHAUER, O.P.

□ 20 □

Our Lady of Guard — Bologna

A common complaint about prayer is: "Oh, I know I should pray, and I would if I could only remember. I always seem to forget."

I once met an army sergeant who found a solution to that problem. He always rebelled at the demand of military courtesy that enlisted men must salute all officers. Every time he had to salute an officer, he decided to whisper a very short prayer to our Blessed Lady. He told me one day:

"Father, you'd be surprised how I've cultivated the habit of prayer by this practice. The practice of saluting is gone now, but the habit of prayer still remains."

The soldier's salute can be easily transferred to a housewife's daily chore of washing the dishes, or answering the phone, or sweeping a floor — to a stenographer filing a letter — to a college man lighting a cigarette. . . . Peter J. Muldoon, *Crusade of Prayers.*

. . .*ever-open Gate of Heaven,*

VOL. I, NO. I, MDV, FEB. 1957

NOVEMBER

□ 21 □

Presentation of the Holy Child Mary in the Temple

This is a feast to set one dreaming. How old was Mary when presented? Why was she presented? What did she do in the Temple? The Apocryphal Gospels answer all such questions. But what are such answers worth?

The mystery of Mary's Presentation is one that we ourselves live. For, at our Baptism, we were presented into the Temple of God which is the Mystical Body of Christ. Therein we are to live as Mary is said to have lived in the Temple of the Old Law: "in retirement, humility, and love," she prepared herself for her incomparable destiny, even as she perfected the prayer of, and for, the entire human race. That is our work of love on earth. It will prepare us for our "presentation" in the Temple of God's Glory which we call heaven.

Let no one of us ever forget that we cannot go to heaven alone!

. . .*Star of the Sea, come to our aid.*

M. RAYMOND, O.C.S.O.

□ 22 □

*Founding of the Confraternity of the Presentation
of Our Lady by St. Omer — 1841*

Mary's place in the Redemption was in the mind of God from all eternity. From all time she was predestined to be the Mother of our Savior. For this reason she was preserved from the taint of original sin, endowed with extraordinary graces, and given the privilege of sharing uniquely in the sufferings and death of Christ.

On November 21, 1964, Pope Paul VI received a standing ovation from the twenty-five hundred bishops attending the Second Vatican Council when he solemnly proclaimed Mary as the Mother of the Church — our spiritual mother.

The Council reaffirmed devotion to Mary in these words: "Let them value highly the pious practices and exercises directed to the Blessed Mother, and approved over the centuries by the Church." We honor her by prayer and confidence in her help, and by imitating her virtues.

. . .*Help the fallen who strive to rise again.*

MAURUS FITZ GERALD, O.F.M.

□ 23 □

Our Lady of the Teutonic House at Jerusalem —
Military Order of Teutonic Knights

Matthew's genealogy of Jesus surprises us by including several foreign women, confirming that gentiles were part of God's intention. Tamar, the Canaanite seductress, is followed by Rahab, the harlot of Jericho. Gentle Ruth, the Moabite, adopted the ways of the Hebrews. Bethsheba, mother of Solomon, is royally counted. Lastly there is the Jewish maiden, the Immaculate Mary, whose fiat verified Paul's words that God predestined "those he foreknew to share the image of His Son, that the Son might be the first-born of many brothers."

The Blessed Virgin moves through the pages of Scripture with a simple nobility, sensitive to the needs of others.

Historian Jacques Bossuet once wrote: "God, who gave Jesus Christ through Mary, does not change His method, style or plan. Mary was Mother of the Head. Mary is Mother of the members." A joy to the Father, spotless spouse of the Spirit, she became tabernacle for the Son. . . .

. . .*While nature marveled,*

MARION EGAN

□ 24 □

Our Lady of Montserrat — Spain

"The Most Holy Virgin was the providential instrument chosen by the designs of the Heavenly Father to give and present His precious Son to the world" — Pope Pius XII, in Demarest and Taylor, *The Dark Virgin.*

Christian devotion through the ages has given Mary many titles of devotion. Saints like Bernard and Alphonsus have praised her with poetic inspiration. God alone has given her the title which is above any that mere mankind might ever affect — Mother of God. The Church has solemnly defined that in a word, *Theotokos,* the God-bearer.

The centuries that preceded the civil rights struggles still do not lack those who championed the cause of the downtrodden. Most often these incidents were involved with the Marian devotion. One of the most striking is that of the "Morenata," the small black statue at the Benedictine Abbey in Catalonia, Spain.

. . . you gave birth to your most holy Creator,

REV. CHARLES DOLLEN

□ 25 □

Our Lady of the Rock — Fiezoli, Tuscany

"Our tainted nature's solitary boast," is the way the English poet laureate William Wordsworth spoke of Mary. He was not a Catholic and yet he knew she was the greatest human God ever made. Long before any movements for women began, the Church honored Mary as the greatest saint in heaven.

If God came on earth in the form of a servant and creature, why may not His Mother rise to be a Queen? And so she is. If men sought the Apostles to speak to Christ for them, how much more so should we seek to have His Mother speak for us.

God meant in the beginning to walk with man in the world, but man rejected Him. And so He had to choose another way. he came to a young maiden in the little village of Nazareth and, by means of an angel, asked if He might come into the world again through her. All nature held its breath for her reply. The first man said "no" to God, but Mary without hesitation said "yes." Why shouldn't we love her then with all our hearts? For it was by means of Mary that we have been reunited to God, our Father.

. . .before and after still a virgin.

REV. RAWLEY MYERS

□ 26 □

Our Lady of the Mountains — Mount Esquilin, Italy

The people of the world also suffered in 1917. Our Lady had appeared to the children at Fatima on the thirteenth of each month starting in May. August 13 was an exception, however, because they had been kidnapped and jailed in Ourem. Our Lady appeared to them after their return home, to Valinhos, on August 19.

Fatima is unpretentious. A mountain landscape adds beauty where simplicity and truth abound. Celestial apparitions revealed she was the Mother of God. Mary gave the children various counsels for the future. Fatima's message spread far and wide, crossing the frontiers of Portugal. Pilgrims came in crowds. Fatima, considered the most famous sanctuary to our Lady in the world, is a place of worship.

"Men must amend their lives and ask pardon for their sins. Men must no longer offend our Lord, who is already offended too much." This was the message of penance by our Lady. It asks us not only to repent for past sins, but to expiate them with faith, to break away from sin completely, for sin offends Almighty God and deeply grieves Him.

. . .*Now hear again the angel's greeting*

MARIE LAYNE

□ 27 □

Our Lady of the Miraculous Medal — Children of Mary

There are many symbols that remind us of our Lady. Many favors have been granted to those who wear the Miraculous Medal and other symbols blessed in honor of the Blessed Virgin. Each symbol in itself means nothing, unless our thoughts and actions are centered on the fairest, purest, brightest, rarest, and dearest person, who always waits for our urgent prayer petitions and our needful pleas. No great sorrow or unusual need is denied when our hearts are full of love and respect for the one who is the Mother of all.

Our Lady of the Miraculous Medal, we invite you into our lives. Dear Mother, we seek the love of your Son, Jesus. Your great intercession has been proven, many times, through the years. We seek your unique confidence and tender consolation, and hope through your efforts, that Jesus can come into our lives and fill it with grace.

. . .*and show your compassion for sinners.*

JOHN JULIUS FISHER

NOVEMBER

□ 28 □

Our Lady of Walsingham — England

The presence of Mary is in Catholic life. "One in thy thousand statues we salute thee," wrote G. K. Chesterton. The thousand and one shrines giving her titles are as varied as the geography of the Church and reflecting the nations, races, and cultures that make up the Catholic community.

From Our Lady of Walsingham in England to Our Lady of Guadalupe in Mexico; from the jewel-adorned Madonna on Russian icons to the black Virgins of Uganda and Biafra; from the classical shrines like Lourdes and Fatima to the roadside shrines of Quebec, Poland, and Austria. . . . All reflect a common faith, a common devotion, and an ancient Catholic conviction about the Mother of God.

In Mary, at every stage of history, the Christian sees his better face and she sums up for us all that is noblest and best. He who is mighty has done great things for her, and she, in turn, continues to do great things for those who recognize her as the Mother of God and Help of Christians.

. . . Lord, into your hands I commend my spirit.

REV. CLIFFORD STEVENS

□ 29 □

Our Lady of the Crown — Palermo, Italy

The calender once listed this day as the feast of St. Saturninus, about whom we know very little. It is noteworthy, also on this day, there died a holy Franciscan who was very devoted to Mary as the Immaculate Conception. Blessed Francis Anthony of Lucera is his name. He was beatified in 1951.

More than a century before our Lady appeared at Lourdes and announced that she was the Immaculate Conception, Francis Anthony had the whole town of Lucera in Apulia making a novena to Mary Immaculate every year. He died on the day of that novena in 1742.

This "Blessed" was commonly called "Johnnie" in his early years. To the many "Johnnies" in our land we can give nothing better than a devotion to Mary Immaculate and a consciousness that there is a "Communion of Saints" in which she shared.

. . .Grant me a quiet night and a worthy dying at the end of my days.

M. RAYMOND, O.C.S.O.

□ 30 □

Our Lady of Genesta — Genoa, Italy

In response to the angel's message Mary humbly said: "I am the servant of the Lord." Humility was the foundation of her life. It is the basis of all spiritual life. Unfortunately, this virtue is often misunderstood. It does not demand that we make a doormat of ourselves. It does not mean we crawl and grovel with an inferiority complex. This is not virtue. The essence of humility is truth. The truth about ourselves is that we have worth. Mary did not reject the salutation: "Hail, full of grace." She accepted her worth. St. Thomas defines humility as a "reasonable pursuit of one's own excellence."

Mary accepted her worth and acknowledged her good. At the same time she recognized that her worth came from God. She declares: "The most high has done great things to me." Our life too must be a "declaration of dependence" on God for all the good that we have and all the good that we do. This is truth.

. . .May the souls of the faithful departed, through the mercy of God, rest in peace. Amen.

ALBERT J. NIMETH, O.F.M.

NOVEMBER

DECEMBER

□ 1 □

Our Lady of Ratisbon — Bavaria

In his encyclical letter (*Magnae Dei Matria — on the Rosary*) of September 8, 1892, Pope Leo XIII reveals how from his earliest days he had a great love for Mary.

"As time went on it became more and more evident how deserving of love and honor was she whom God Himself was the first to love. He loved so much more than any other that after elevating her high above all the rest of His creation and adorning her with richest gifts, He made her His Mother."

During the long pontificate of Leo XIII our Lady was ever at his side. "Throughout many dreadful events of every kind which the times have brought to pass, always with her have we sought refuge, always to her have we lifted up our intent and ardent eyes." His one desire was that he might be able, in return for Mary's protection and love, to show her the heart of a most devoted son.

To Mary, Our Hope: Mary, hope of the world, hail!

MOST REV. JOHN J. CARBERRY

□ 2 □

Our Lady of Didynia — Cappadocia

In Advent you just can't get away from Mary. Over and over the Church addresses the Christ Child as the "Root of Jesse." The comparison is a good one. Jesse was King David's father and the Christ Child is the direct descendant of David through the family lineage of His Mother Mary.

"The Jews," wrote St. Jerome, "interpret the rod and the flower of the root of Jesse to be the Lord Himself. . .The rod signifies the power of the ruler and the flower designates His beauty. We, however, may understand the rod of the root of Jesse to be the Virgin Mary. . . ."

Mary is also the rod that holds up all of us. In first holding up the flower of the Christ Child who is the Head of the Body which is the Church, Mary becomes for all of us our strongest defender and advocate. O Root of Jesse, who stands for an ensign of the people, before whom kings shall keep silence and to whom the gentiles shall pray — come to deliver us, and tarry now no more.

. . .Hail, gentle, serene, and loving mother.

REV. VINCENT A. YZERMANS

□ 3 □

Our Lady of Filermo;
Our Lady of Victories

With what devotion and fervor should we not recite the Hail Mary which sums up so beautifully all the glories of Mary! It tells us of the reverence and esteem with which the angel greeted her in God's name, and it reminds us constantly of the homage which the Church ever renders her by proclaiming her blessed among women, the Holy Mother of God.

The fervent recitation of this prayer must rejoice the heart of Mary, since it recalls the mystery of the Annunciation, that blessed moment when the Word was made flesh in her virginal bosom, when the Son of God became in truth and forever her own beloved Son. And what joy should it not bring to our own hearts, since it reminds us of that moment in which Mary became not only the Mother of God but our Mother as well! — V. Rev. A. Tanquerey, S.S., *Doctrine and Devotion.*

. . . Holy Mother of Jesus Christ, you alone were chosen to be

G. JOSEPH GUSTAFSON, S.S.

□ 4 □

Madonna of Holy Purity

Conjugal chastity has always been part of married life in the Church. This sacredness has been heralded by Holy Mary, Mother Most Chaste. The sacred purpose of a Catholic marriage is to be faithful to spouse and to cooperate with God in the propagation of the human race. This always has been a tenet of the Church.

The poisons of unfaithfulness, abuse, and sexual deviation have caused the marriage institution to suffer. Many partners in marriage, as well as their children, have experienced the pains and hardships created by occasional sins that would cause gaps and chasms in spiritual lives.

When petitioned, Mother Most Chaste has interceded for many needful persons, who by prayers and devotions have found new hope by seeking Mary's help. Once more, the presence of God entered their married life, and love began to blossom again.

. . . his maiden mother and his source of nourishment.

JOHN JULIUS FISHER

□ 5 □

Virgin Most Powerful

What a happy way to enter the next world! Simeon declares with unspeakable joy and faith: "Now, Master, you can dismiss your servant in peace!" We will not have to envy his holy departure if we recite thoughtfully the words in the Hail Mary: "Pray for us sinners now, and at the hour of our death." We have repeated them so often that these words may not really register. We can be numbed by repetition.

By asking the Mother of God to pray for us because of our sinful condition, we acknowledge our blameworthiness with humility. This is so pleasing to her that she obtains pardon and forgiveness for us from her Divine Son. When the time comes to render an account of our stewardship, Mary will spread her protective cloak over us to ward off the last-minute attacks by the evil one. Ours will be a happy death! "Never was it known that anyone. . . ."

   . . .*Empress of angels, comforter of sinners,*

BRUCE RISKI, O.F.M. Cap.

□ 6 □

Notre Dame de Fourviere — Lyons, France

Once the Word became flesh in Mary, she was fired by His presence to do for others. Carrying her God who had leaped down from the everlasting hills, Mary went up into the Judean hill country to help Elizabeth. At her glad approach to embrace her cousin, little John leaped for joy in his mother's womb.

Jesus had already shown the magnetism of His presence. Later He would do it to Magdalen, to the woman with the issue of blood, to the Samaritan woman at Jacob's well. . . .

We who carry Christ within us cannot sit smug and content at home. Like our Lady we too must answer to Christ within us. Out to the "hill country," humming our Magnificat, we must carry Christ's love to those who need us most: the depressed, the worried, the unpopular, the dull.

   . . .*come to my aid, console me, a sinner.*

REV. ROBERT L. WILKEN

□ 7 □

Vigil of the Immaculate Conception

One of the first American Catholic Chaplains to be lost in the Second World War was the Rev. Aloysius H. Schmidt of the Archdiocese of Dubuque. Father Schmidt died a heroic death aboard the USS Oklahoma, during the bombing of Pearl Harbor on December 7, 1941.

As the Oklahoma sank, Father Schmidt, who had done everything he could to help the other sailors to be saved, was trapped in one of the cabins. He was last seen looking from the porthole and waving his hand while holding the rosary. In a few moments the waves had swallowed him and thus he met his God His thoughts must have been directed to our Lady as he solved the mystery of life.

If we pray the Rosary and love the Rosary in life, we may confidently trust that we shall be blessed by our Lady's presence at the hour of our death.

. . .*Queen of heaven, I ask but one favor of you:*

MOST REV. JOHN J. CARBERRY

□ 8 □

The Immaculate Conception of the Blessed Virgin Mary
(Patronal Feast of the United States of America since 1846)

Today we celebrate the moment in which began the existence of the Blessed Virgin and, at the same time, the high privilege that Mary had, unique among all men, of being preserved, through the merits of Jesus Christ, from all stain of original sin.

Today's feast is not, in its origin and principle, in relation to Advent: it was set on the eighth day of December to complete the period of nine months before Mary's birth (September 8). However, we can easily find a connection between this feast and the spirit of Advent: while we await the Savior and we feel the need of the Redeemer, we turn our gaze toward the Redeemer's Mother, and today's feast becomes the aurora which precedes the Son of Christmas. Thus today is a real Advent feast.

. . .*that you pray for my forgiveness, standing before the throne*

REV. MSGR. THOMAS J. TOBIN

□ 9 □

Our Lady of the Conception — Naples, Italy

Our Lady's beauty must make us pause in wondering contemplation. Knowing her, we discover more fully how our faith forms us in joy and peace. In the plan of God, the Jewish people were chosen to be the vehicle of salvation for the entire world. The glory of Israel is a poor maiden, hidden in the obscurity of a Palestinian town, the culmination of all the yearnings of mankind for union with God.

Flooded from the first moment of her existence with the Spirit of God, Mary freely and spontaneously yields to God's love: "Behold the handmaid of the Lord; be it done to me according to your will." Christ comes at Mary's loving "Yes!" In our Advent preparations for Christmas, we can sweep away the negatives in our life. We must yield to God and say "Yes!" to His life of grace.

. . .of your Son, whose justice rightly awakens fear in me.

REV. MSGR. FRANCIS TOURNIER

□ 10 □

Translation of the House of Loreto

In reciting the Litany of Our Lady we invoke Mary as "Queen of the Most Holy Rosary." Pope Leo XIII placed this invocation in the Litany of his letter of December 24, 1883.

"To the honor, therefore, of Mary, the great Mother of God, for a perpetual remembrance of the prayer for her protection offered among all nations throughout the month of October to her most pure heart; as an enduring testimony of the unbounding trust which we put in our most loving Mother, and in order that we may day by day, more and more obtain her favorable aid: we will and decree that in the Litany of Loreto, after the invocation, 'Queen conceived without Original Sin,' shall be added the suffrage, 'Queen of the Most Holy Rosary, Pray for us.' "

O Mary, my Queen and my Mother, help me to know the Rosary, to love the Rosary, and to say it daily.

. . .O Virgin Mary, be not far from me, for you are full of grace.

MOST REV. JOHN J. CARBERRY

□ 11 □

Madonna of the Angels — Livry Forest, near Paris

The angel who announced to Zachary he was to have a son in his old age, and who gently asked Mary if she were willing to be the Mother of God, is the last angel whose name we have on record — Gabriel. In Hebrew, this name means "Hero of God!" The Jews revered him as an angel of judgment. Mohammedans believe he was the mouthpiece of God dictating the Koran.

I live near Holy Cross Abbey, in Colorado, and it is such a joy to hear the monastery bells ring out the hours, especially the Angelus. Gabriel is remembered in this prayer, developed during the 1300s, for the word means "The angel. . . ."

In the picture "Our Lady of Perpetual Help," two angels are painted to the left of Mary's head. Gabriel is thought to be the one holding the cross. An angel came to strengthen Christ at Gethsemane and tradition has it he was Gabriel. Perhaps he was Christ's special ministering angel.

. . .*Be the guardian of my heart,*

JEANNE DAGEFORDE

□ 12 □

Our Lady of Guadalupe — Mexico

Four centuries ago an Indian, Juan Diego, encountered at Tepeyac, near Mexico City, a maiden who spoke his language. She asked him to visit the bishop and tell him that she was the Mother of God and wished a church to be built in her honor at Tepeyac.

The bishop, naturally, asked for a sign that the maiden really was the Virgin Mary. Later, she folded roses in Juan's blanket and told him to give them to the bishop "as a sign." When the blanket unrolled before the prelate he fell on his knees before a colored picture of the Blessed Virgin, imprinted on the blanket. A church was built and the blanket has been displayed for four centuries, although most similar blankets disintegrate in forty years. Eight million Indians were converted in seven years at the same time that millions of Catholics were quitting the Church in Europe.

We should pray in thanksgiving to her whom Pope Paul called: "Patroness of the Americas."

. . .*seal me with a fitting fear of God, and guide me in steadfast ways.*

JOHN M. MARTIN, M.M.

□ 13 □

Our Lady of the Holy Chapel — Paris

The Church Year is very subtle. Advent reminds us that Jesus was in the world long before Christmas day. Mary was the tabernacle. She had her Son in a closer union than she would ever have Him again. The kingdom of God was within her!

DECEMBER

Unlike Mary we see through the glass darkly; are one with the song-writer calling for a dove to carry him away to a place of rest; the pilgrim retracing the footsteps of Christ in Palestine; the poet seeking God in nature, the philosopher in words and theories.

Those who search for love, of God, neighbor, and self, no longer look through the glass darkly, but like Mary find the kingdom of God within themselves.

. . .Give me the grace to avoid sin and to cherish all that is good.

ANNE TANSEY

□ 14 □

Our Lady of Albe la Royale — Hungary

Mary gave God lips to announce the consoling tidings that the "kingdom of God was at hand." They called man to penance and urged all to take up the cross. They taught lessons of love and inspired all those who heard Him speak "as no man spoke before." With these lips God affirmed the weak and praised the good, where He found it and little good where He found no more. "The bruised reed he did not break and the smoking flax he did not extinguish.

"Peace. Be of good cheer. Take heart. Fear not. Your sins are forgiven. Neither will I condemn you. May your joy be filled. Judge not and you will not be jduged." These are the kinds of words that came from the lips of God.

Like Mary we can give God lips — our lips — to bring His message to the world, to instruct the ignorant, counsel the doubtful, solace the bereaved, encourage the fainthearted, and bolster the insecure.

. . .O gentle Virgin, among those born of women, there has been none other like you.

ALBERT J. NIMETH, O.F.M.

□ 15 □

Octave of the Immaculate Conception

It was always the common teaching of the Church that the Blessed Virgin Mary was the most perfect human being created by God.

In 1854 Pope Pius IX declared Mary to have been conceived without original sin. Four years later in visions to a poor little girl of Lourdes, Bernadette Soubirous, Mary identified herself by saying, "I am the Immaculate Conception."

The sacrament of Baptism removed the stain of original sin from us, but the effects of this sin have remained in our human nature, making us prone to succumb to sin, faults, and imperfections. In our struggle to do good and avoid evil, let us pray to Mary.

. . .The Creator of all chose you to be his Mother.

PASCHAL BOLAND, O.S.B.

□ 16 □

Confraternity of Our Lady of Deliverance in France — 1583

"Let us be in haste to give Jesus to the people." — Mother Teresa, Rochester, Minnesota, 1976.

It somehow seems incongruous to see the security guard at O'Hare Airport rifle thorugh Mother Teresa's old, gray, carry-on sack. She would be the least likely suspect for carrying a bomb. The guard would be more likely to find a holy picture, a book, or small statue of our Blessed Mother. Being devoted to Mary, Mother Teresa has shown her devotion in many ways. If presented with a bouquet, her first impulse is to place it before an image of Mary as a token of love.

Mother Teresa claims that the most beautiful thing about Mary was that when Jesus came into her life, she immediately, in haste, went to St. Elizabeth's home to give Jesus to her and John the Baptist. And we read in the Gospel that the child leapt with joy at this first contact with Christ.

Let us be in haste to share the Good News, to give Jesus to the people.

. . .He cleansed Magdalene from sin;

ALICE COLLINS

DECEMBER

□ 17 □

Our Lady of Amiens — France

A most touching incident in the life of our Lady, recounted in Scripture, is her visit to her cousin Elizabeth. Mary "makes haste" to tend her cousin in childbearing, even as she herself bears Christ within. Mary reached out in unselfish love to one of her own family. She did not hesitate, considering her own condition. She saw a need, and rushed to alleviate it. Family ties are loosening today as never before. Homes become mere hotels; family relationships often deteriorate into a shambles of self-centeredness.

This Christmas, some will merely go through the motions of family peace, "for the children's sake." For our own sake, we need to pray during this season that our family unity, even across distances, will be sincere and deep.

. . .now, at your prayer, may he likewise wash away my sins

REV. MSGR. FRANCIS TOURNIER

□ 18 □

Expectation of the Blessed Virgin Mary

The visit of the Angel Gabriel to Mary was cause for her reply: "Behold the handmaid of the Lord; be it done to me according to thy word!" This beautiful scene is cause for our witnessing the vocation of Mary — God's call to her to become the Mother of His Son — and her acceptance of her vocation.

On our way to Christmas we pause to reflect on the reason behind it all — why did God become one of us? This feast which acknowledges the utter sinlessness of Mary helps us to be the realist in assessing our own condition: our strength is weakness, our stature insignificant, our years swiftly spent. We can see so much more than we are. Our yearning seems drawn to impossible goals like life beyond death, joy without tears, love without loss. We long to be free, but hunger, anxiety, and death mock our prayer.

Mary is victory, Mary is complete goodness. God exempted her so that His promise to us might take flesh. Mary is not an awesome queen who is most unlikely to give us an audience. She is a mother, and whoever heard of a mother hard to approach?

. . .and preserve me from the depths of hell.

REV. RALPH C. HARTMAN

DECEMBER

□ 19 □

Our Lady of Etalem — Bavaria

"Hail, our life, our sweetness, and our hope!"

When we speak of our Lady as "our life" we mean just that. Through her fiat at the Annunciation she made it possible for the Second Person of the Blessed Trinity to come into the world to save men from their sins. Eternal life is ours because of the cooperation of Mary with God's plan. Even our life in this twentieth century is made bearable because so many of our values rest on Western Christian civilization of which she is one of the cornerstones.

Moreover, she is our "sweetness and our hope." Her physical and spiritual beauty bring joy to every heart. Refinement always follows her. Persons will not be dejected or depressed for long when they realize that their heavenly Mother loves and cares for them.

. . .*O thornless Rose, healing power on behalf of sinners,*

EDWIN R. MC DEVITT, M.M.

□ 20 □

Notre Dame de Molem

With all of the privileges and titles that belong to the Blessed Virgin Mary, none is more meaningful than "Mother of God." Because God Himself chose her first, all the other titles that Christian devotion can give are rightfully hers.

Mary is the first Christian. Her response to the Angel Gabriel's "Ave!" came from a heart full of faith, hope, and love. All the longing faith of the Old Testament was brought to fulfillment in her reply. But, she was the first human being to believe in Christ and put that belief to work.

What must have been the thoughts of her heart as she prepared for the first Christmas. As she fashioned those swaddling clothes and packed them for the trip to Bethlehem, her heart must have been elevated to a most perfect union with God. Mary, the first Christian, is indeed blessed among women.

. . .*call on God to protect me in this earthly storm.*

REV. CHARLES DOLLEN

DECEMBER

◻ 21 ◻

Notre Dame de St. Acheul

Pope Paul VI wrote a special letter under date of March 12, 1964, to Father Patrick Peyton, C.S.C., commending the Family Rosary.

"The unity and sanctity of the family, today so gravely and so universally threatened and attacked, will find their sure defense and unfailing protection in the practice of family prayer. As the motto of the Family Crusade succinctly asserts: The Family that prays together, stays together; and this unity will be a holy one, founded on the raising of the mind and heart to God in the meditation of the mysteries of the life, death and resurrection of Our Divine Redeemer and the life of His Immaculate Mother.

"We therefore warmly recommend the Family Rosary Crusade, which inculcates the practice of daily prayer, of family prayer, and of prayer by means of the Rosary, in which 'meditating upon these mysteries. . . we may both imitate what they contain and obtain what they promise.' " — Mass for feast of the Most Holy Rosary.

. . .*O Christ, the mighty Father's Son,*

MOST REV. JOHN J. CARBERRY

◻ 22 ◻

Notre Dame de Chartres

Mary and Hannah had this in common: both had very special pregnancies and both had sons who were prophets. Hannah beseeched God for a son whom she would give back to God, as soon as he would be weaned. She fulfilled her promise. Her fidelity sparks a question within me: Am I as earnest in thanking God for answered prayers as I am in the asking? Do I carry out everything I told God I would do as proof of my sincerity?

Mary's conviction that God could and would do whatever He said welled up so within her that it found expression in her *Magnificat*, her high praise of God. All the glory is *His*. Mary was fed well by the Spirit; her praise is quite similar to that prayed by Hannah (1 Samuel 2.1-10). The "meat" of their praise is their dependence on the love, providence, power, and wisdom of their God.

. . .*remembering the Mother who bore you and nourished you,*

SISTER THERESA MOLPHY, C.S.J.

☐ 23 ☐

Our Lady of Dardilliers — Anjou, France

The United States of America was dedicated to Mary Immaculate in 1846. In times of crisis, a mother rushes to her offspring. Mary often acts as the spiritual mother of many persons in need. She does not need a second request; her spiritual ways are offered immediately to all in our country.

Sincere humble petitions to Mary, devotions in her honor, and Rosaries offered to receive interceding help are the basic methods used by her adopted children of America to receive her blessings.

Our lives become more meaningful and take on a special purpose when we seek aid and intervention through Mary Immaculate. In the past, she has responded wholeheartedly to the American people's request. We need her positive attitude to frame new goals and new methods to make our country strong, vibrant, and prosperous.

. . .grant me salvation of body and soul.

JOHN JULIUS FISHER

☐ 24 ☐

Nuptials of the Virgin Mary with St. Joseph

To arrive at a true idea of the dignity of St. Joseph, we take for granted appreciation of the true dignity of Mary. God certainly did not choose an unworthy man to be the husband of the virgin Mother of God, linked so closely to the mystery of God becoming man. Joseph's position with respect to our Lady is "conceded to St. Joseph by the singular gift of God and by a dispensation that surpasses all understanding."

Probably the best summary of this is found in Pope Leo XIII's encyclical, *Quamquam Pluries.* "The dignity of the Mother of God is certainly so sublime that nothing can surpass it. Nonetheless, since the bond of marriage existed between Joseph and the Blessed Virgin, there can be no doubt that more than any other person he approached that supereminent dignity by which the Mother of God is raised far above all created natures." — Francis L. Filas, S.J., S.T.D., *Joseph Most Just.*

. . .Wipe away my sins; create in me a pure heart.

G. JOSEPH GUSTAFSON, S.S.

☐ 25 ☐

Jesus Born of the Virgin Mary

That He became man as a tiny, helpless baby, this is the wonder of it. He could have come in all His majesty but He chose to come as a little baby.

So often the nativity scenes are untrue to the wonderful reality. They make the Infant a big child, looking almost as if He could speak. But the truth is far more wonderful. He was a tiny bit of humanity, completely helpless in His Mother's arms.

How can we help but love Mary. God loved her so much that He placed in her arms and in her care His only-begotten Son. This is the baby who has come to redeem the world, this is our Savior. This tiny little baby is true God and true man. He who will help us all, who will open the gates of heaven for us, is a helpless little infant in His Mother's arms.

. . .Grant me sure hope, right faith, perfect charity,

DALE FRANCIS

☐ 26 ☐

The Archiropita — Rossano, Italy
(Byzantine fresco of the Madonna in Cathedral of Assunta)

The first days of our Blessed Savior on earth were days of great joy for Mary. She had given birth to a Son. The Babe she held in her arms was none other than her God and her Creator, but at the same time, flesh of her flesh. There ran in His veins her own most pure blood.

Exempt from all the pain and weakness which is the lot of all other mothers since the sin of Eve, Mary was, from the first moment, able to bring to Jesus all the care and attention that His helplessness, as a new-born child, needed. Every service that His infant state demanded of her was promptly and lovingly provided.

To feel God powerless in one's arms and to be able to minister to His wants would be enough to bewilder any soul less strong and less simple than Mary's. Her motherly attentions to her Child were her worship.

. . .and the grace beyond every other —

THOMAS M. BREW, S.J.

☐ 27 ☐

Founding of the Order of the Knights of Our Lady — 1370

I plead for a religion in which the Babe of Christmas is not an orphan, but a Child of Mary. I plead for a religion which breathes respect for motherhood, and vibrates with a love for that Mother, above all mothers, who brought our Savior into the world. If there is any man or woman looking for a test as to what constitutes the divine religion on this earth, let him apply the same test he would to the judgment of man. If you ever want to know the real qualities of a man, judge him not by his attitude on the world of commerce, his outlook on business, his kindness and his genteel manners, but judge him by his attitude to his mother.

If you want to know the quality of a religion, judge it exactly the same way, that is, by the attitude that it bears to the Mother of our blessed Lord. If you find a religion which never speaks of that Woman who gave us our Redeemer, then there certainly must be something wanting to the truth of that religion, and — even to its humanity.

. . .*a holy death.*

MOST REV. FULTON J. SHEEN

☐ 28 ☐

Notre Dame de Pontoise

There is a story as to how the words "*Maria Regina Mater,*" freely translated, "*Mary, my Queen and my Mother,*" came to have a special meaning for the writer.

One of the pleasant tasks of a newly named bishop is the choosing of a motto for his episcopal coat of arms. Suggestions were offered by brother priests of one which would express devotion to our Lady.

The title of the new Mass for the Queenship of Mary which was first celebrated in May of 1956, the month of my designation as bishop-elect, offered one which was reassuring, namely, "*Maria Regina,*" *(Mary Queen)*. To this was added the simple word "*Mater*" *(Mother)* and the motto was completed.

While "*Maria Regina*" honors the Queenship of Mary, the loving word "*Mater*" added so much more, namely, the divine motherhood of our Blessed Mother and her spiritual motherhood of us.

. . .*Death may take my body,*

MOST REV. JOHN J. CARBERRY

DECEMBER

☐ 29 ☐

Our Lady of Spire — Germany

One Christmas Eve a little boy sauntered to the crib in a crowded church and vigorously sang, "Happy Birthday" to Jesus.

After all, it *was* Christ's birthday, so why not be happy for Him? That is the magical delight about those small creatures called children. They are proud of being alive, and want the whole world to know it.

Their songs, their delights, their unexpected sayings and their happiness — all these are reasons why children are such wonderful things. It is a pity that more parents do not *enjoy* their children. So many spend so much of their time correcting and disciplining and screaming at their children that the overall effect of obedience is lost. Love and discipline certainly are necessary factors, but we beg you parents, try *enjoying* your children a bit more.

Find your happiness with, and for them; it will be a deep joy, modeled after the Holy Family's love and mutual help for each other in Nazareth.

. . .but let no other death come near me.

PETER V. ROGERS, O.M.I.

☐ 30 ☐

Our Lady of Boulogne — Picardy, France;
Feast of the Holy Family

Family life can and should be beautiful, yet many times family life in the day-to-day living can present many difficulties. In celebrating the feast of the Holy Family we not only acknowledge the family life of Jesus, Mary, and Joseph but realize the importance and value of Christian family life today.

The section from Sirach deals with the relationship between parents and children and the respect and care to be expected from children. "He who honors his father is gladdened by children. . .he stores up riches who reveres his mother." Children today should heed this message.

In the Gospel account of the finding of Jesus we see a mother's love and concern not to be forgotten, as we are told: "Mary kept these things in her memory." Lord, that we may in some way imitate the Holy Family in our daily family life, for this we pray.

. . .In my resurrection, my eyes shall then behold you,

SISTER CAROL ANN KENZ, C.S.J.

□ 31 □

Our Lady of the Closing Year

"Imagine the joy of holding the Christ Child in your arms," a woman said as she studied a picture of Mary, Joseph, and the Child. "It would be a terrible responsibility," her husband replied. "In holding Christ you would be holding all mankind. You would be committing yourself totally, and have no time for yourself."

Doesn't this happen when we receive Holy Communion? The Eucharistic union means being Christ's hands and feet, finding the lost sheep, feeding the hungry, denouncing discrimination, binding up wounds, spreading the Word of God, and looking out for "the least" of Christ's people.

We are about to face another year, another chance to make up for all those lost ones when we didn't understand.

. . .and I shall remain forever with you. Amen.

— adapted from a prayer attributed to Pope Innocent III

ANNE TANSEY

DECEMBER